To Allan,
Best ...

JOHN SIN
KIRKPATRICK

The Untold Story of the
Gallipoli Hero's Early Life

JIM MULHOLLAND

ALKALI PUBLISHING

Published in 2015 by Alkali Publishing.

www.alkalipublishing.com

Copyright © Jim Mulholland 2015

ISBN 978 0 9933457 0 8

Printed and bound in the UK by CVN Print Ltd, 42 Maxwell Street, South Shields, Tyne & Wear NE33 4PU.

CONTENTS

PREFACE

I have been aware of the story of John Simpson Kirkpatrick, 'The Man with the Donkey' at Gallipoli, since my childhood. Yet it was only a chance conversation with a complete stranger at South Shields Central Library that made me delve into the history of the town's most famous son. Once I embarked upon the task I was completely hooked and with each new discovery my interest deepened. That was nine years ago and I can honestly say my enthusiasm has never waned in all that time.

The aim of this book is to tell the story of his early life on Tyneside, prior to leaving for Australia and being caught up in the maelstrom of the First World War. The book contains many unpublished stories, documents and photographs. It also features unedited transcripts of the correspondence between him and his family during his first sea voyage. Finally, I examine the aftermath of his death and how his memory was kept alive by family members, friends and various institutions in his home town.

The conclusions reached are based on factual evidence found during the course of my extensive research and on my own assumptions cross-referenced with evidence taken from various key sources: principally the living descendants of the Kirkpatrick/Simpson families and the people who knew him; census returns; certificates of births, deaths and marriages; recently discovered school records including log books; unpublished shipping agreements; military records; previously written books and the archive of the Shields Gazette.

I am, of course, responsible for the content of this book and the views expressed are entirely mine, with any errors being my sole responsibility.

Jim Mulholland

February 2015

GLOSSARY

Aft – towards the stern or rear section of a ship.

Auld – a Scottish word meaning old.

Bob – a shilling (s), equivalent to 12 old pennies (d).

Brig – a sailing vessel with two square rigged masts.

Bunkering/Bunkers – the process of a supplying a ship with coal for its own use.

Canny – a slang word meaning good or nice.

Charabanc – a group day out on a tram or bus.

Chandler – a dealer in special supplies or equipment for ships.

Chuck – slang word for being paid off or dismissed.

Collier - a ship designed to carry coal.

Dodger – a slang word for an old three-penny coin.

Ducket – a wooden structure for keeping pigeons in.

Geordie – someone who hails from the banks of the River Tyne in the North East of England.

Locust Beans – North African Corob tree pods or peas used as a substitute for cocoa powder and to sweeten foods.

Lugger – a small vessel rigged with a lugsail.

Mate – an officer on a ship. The 1st Mate (or Chief Mate) is second in command to the Captain.

Master Mariner – a qualified captain or skipper of a ship, sometimes referred to as 'the old man'.

Nowt – a slang word meaning nothing.

Pit – slang word for a coal mine or colliery.

Plater – a tradesman who works with metal plate.

Pattern Maker – a carpenter, who makes accurate wooden patterns from which steel structures are made.

Quart – a quarter of a gallon or two pints.

Quid – an old pound note (equivalent to 20 shillings).

Stoker – a ship's fireman who shovels coal into the furnace of a vessel's boiler.

Strokes – a slang word meaning hours or time.

Tanner – a slang word for an old silver sixpence.

Tonnage – a measure of the cargo carrying capacity of a ship.

Tons – the old imperial measure of weight.

Tick – a slang word for credit or 'on account'.

Tinty – a slang word for a Chinese person.

Yard – a school playground. Also the old imperial measure of distance, equivalent to 3 feet (ft).

Wack – a slang word meaning share.

Westoe – an old township, which was merged with the township of South Shields to form the town of South Shields.

ABBREVIATIONS

AIF – Australian Imperial Force.

ANZAC – Australian & New Zealand Army Corps.

ONE

THE MAN WITH THE DONKEY

On 19th May 1915 a stretcher bearer from South Shields in the North East of England was killed at Gallipoli. A year earlier the 21 year old bachelor, who went by the name of John Simpson Kirkpatrick, was a stoker on a merchant ship. After three years working the Australian coastline John, known as Jack, was homesick. He wrote to his mother saying "start looking your best" since he was saving up for his passage home to "Canny Auld Shields". However, in August 1914 his ship steamed into the port of Fremantle and he was astounded to discover Britain and her Empire were at war with Germany. Without a doubt Jack saw this as an opportunity for a free ticket home. His plan was to enlist in the Australian Army, thinking he would be sent to England for his basic training. Jack could then visit his mother and sister before embarkation to the Western Front. He jumped ship and 'joined up' using the name John Simpson and due to his muscular physique was selected as a stretcher bearer in the Medical Corps. Jack wrote to his mother informing her of his enlistment as Private J. Simpson (No. 202), confident he'd be home within a few months. However, much to his dismay the Australian and New Zealand troops (later known as the ANZAC's) were sent to Egypt for their training. Jack was devastated and wrote home from Cairo expressing his disappointment, "I would not have joined this contingent if I had known that they were not going to England." On 25th April 1915 the ANZAC's took part in the 'hell hole' that was Gallipoli, a disastrous attempt to knock Germany's ally Turkey out of the war.

Jack's mother Sarah learnt of her son's death in the cruelest of ways, when a letter from his sister Annie was returned from Gallipoli unopened. It had one word written on the outside of the envelope 'killed'. Sarah was devastated and the pain of her loss was witnessed by a nine year old girl called Bessie Hails. A ball she was playing with went into the backyard of Jack's mother's house and she asked to retrieve it. Sarah replied, "Yes, you can have your ball, you can have anything you like. I've just learned that my son's been killed and nothing else matters to me anymore." Following the arrival of another letter at Gallipoli written by Annie, an officer from Jack's unit wrote to her with the details of his heroic death.

September 2nd, 1915
Gallipoli Peninsula

Dear Miss Simpson,

I was extremely sorry to hear from you that you had no word from us about your brother. Colonel Sutton, then commanding the Ambulance wrote, I am practically certain, very shortly after the occurrence. Colonel Sutton has now left us, and I was more in touch with your brother than the other remaining officers of our corps, so I am replying to your letter.

Your brother landed with us from the torpedo boat at daybreak on the 25th of April so taking part in the historic landing. He did excellent work during the day. He discovered a donkey in a deserted hut, took possession, and worked up and down a dangerous valley carrying wounded men to the beach on the donkey. This plan was a very great success, so he continued day by day from morning till night and became one of the best known men in the division. Everyone from the general downwards seems to have known him and his donkey which he christened Murphy. The valley at the time was very dangerous as it was exposed to snipers, and also was continuously shelled. He scorned the danger, and always kept going whistling and singing, a universal favourite. So he worked for three weeks. On the night of the 18th, as you will have read in the papers, the Turks made a heavy attack on our position. Early in the morning as usual your brother was at work, when a Turkish machine-gun played on the track where he was passing, the days of his miraculous escapes were passed, for he fell on the spot shot through the heart. He truly died doing his duty. We buried him that night on a little hill near the sea shore known as Queensland Point, Chaplain-Colonel Green of our division reading the service.

The work your brother did was so exceptionally good that his name was mentioned in orders of the day. We hoped that one of the military decorations of honour might be awarded him, as he fully deserved it, but unfortunately all who deserve cannot receive the special rewards. Mrs. Simpson and yourself can at least take comfort that he gave his life in the performance of gallant and dutiful service that has been excelled by none.

Your brother's effects have been sent to the Base and will be forwarded in due course to you. In conclusion I wish to express the deep sympathy of our whole unit with Mrs. Simpson and yourself in your sad bereavement. Believe me.

Yours Sincerely,

H. Kenneth Fry, Capt.,

3rd. Field Ambulance.

In the wake of his death 'Private Simpson - The Man with the Donkey' quickly obtained hero status in the Australian Press. The Gallipoli landings were a disaster and with nothing but bad news to report his compassionate story took on a life of its own and he was reputed to have saved hundreds of lives. The Gallipoli Campaign resulted in over 140,000 allied casualties and ended in a humiliating withdrawal after an eight month stalemate. Nevertheless, it heralded the birth of two new nations Australia and New Zealand onto the world stage. It gave rise to what became known as the 'ANZAC Spirit' of courage in the face of adversity, endurance and mateship; virtues which have defined the Australian and New Zealand national character for a century.

In recent years some historians and writers have called into question Jack's heroism since his story was seized upon for its propaganda value. However, the passing of time has not diminished his status as Gallipoli's most famous ANZAC. Five states in Australia have erected statues of 'Simpson' and he's affectionately known to millions as 'The Man with the Donkey'. Jack's image has appeared on commemorative stamps, a bank note, the official ANZAC medallion and numerous books have been written about him. Over the years there have been several attempts to award him a posthumous Victoria Cross, but all to no avail.

TWO

ROBERT AND SARAH'S SECRET PAST

Jack was born on 6th July 1892 in Tyne Dock, a working class part of South Shields. He was one of eight children born to Robert Kirkpatrick and Sarah Simpson, who previously lived in Leith, Scotland. In the autumn of 1886 the couple arrived at Tyne Dock with their eldest daughter Maggie. Unbeknown to Jack and his siblings, they were all illegitimate since their parents never married. The reason being, Robert was already married with three children and if he were to marry Sarah he risked being jailed for bigamy. The couples' need for secrecy explains why Sarah's name is absent from the 1891 and 1901 census returns taken in South Shields. In a further twist to the tale, Sarah had given birth to an illegitimate son prior to meeting Robert and starting a relationship with him.

Robert Kirkpatrick was born on 26th November 1837 in Leith, the port of Edinburgh, on the southern shore of the Firth of Forth. He was a career seaman who travelled the world and in 1881 qualified as a Master Mariner. Twenty years earlier, the 24 year old Robert (a humble merchant seaman) married a 23 year old domestic servant Mary McLean in her home town of North Berwick. Robert was the son of a North Sea Pilot and Mary the daughter of a fisherman. The couple initially settled in Leith and had three sons: Robert (b. 1862), Andrew (b. 1864) and John (b. 1866). Tragically, John died the following year of bronchitis. Over the years the conscientious Robert worked his way through the ranks; obtaining his Certificate of Competence as a Second Mate in 1864 and six years later his First Mate's Certificate.

At the time of the 1871 Census the couple were living in lodgings in Granton, north of Edinburgh, while their sons Robert and Andrew were staying with their maternal grandparents in North Berwick. On 28th September 1873 Mary gave birth to the baby of the family William at her parents home, while her husband was employed as a Chief Mate onboard the SS Fifeshire. Two years later Robert, like other ambitious seamen who wanted to get on in the world, became a Freemason in the Provincial Lodge of Edinburgh. In 1877 he secured a much sought after position as a Chief Mate with the London & Edinburgh Shipping Company, which operated out of Leith. At this time the company's steam ships provided a passenger and cargo service between Edinburgh and London every four days. Their vessels also worked abroad and made frequent voyages to Bilbao, Cadiz and Malaga in Spain. During the following nine years as a mate and master Robert worked on various steam ships of about 1,000 tons including the Marmion, Malvina and Iona. Records show that the company's vessels frequently coaled at Tyne Dock staithes, just over 100 miles away in the North East of England.

Sarah Simpson (b. 1855) was one of at least eight children: Christian, Jane, Sebastian, Ann, Sarah, Martha, Julia and Helen. She and her siblings were born in Malaga (as British subjects) to a Scottish father James Simpson and a Welsh mother Ann Simpson (nee Hosgood). James was an engine fitter whose skills in the new industrial age of steam power were much in demand abroad. It would appear he had a head for business and the family prospered. Many years later Sarah would tell her daughter Maggie that her father James owned a gun cartridge factory and a small vineyard for the making of port wine. Sarah had an idyllic childhood. She was brought up in a villa with servants and was educated by a governess.

Sadly, by the time of the 1871 Census the Simpson's had returned to Scotland due to a down turn in the family's fortune. They were living at Gloucester Street in Glasgow and Sarah's father was recorded as being 'unemployed'. Their neighbours included a grain merchant and a master baker, which suggests that James Simpson still had some savings. However, the need to bring money into the household was paramount and the pampered life style of the Simpson siblings was a thing of the past. Sarah's brother Sebastian (aged 20) was following in his father's footsteps working as an engine fitter at a local engineering works; Christian (aged 24) was a milliner; Jane (aged 23) and Ann (aged 18) were employed as dressmakers; while Martha (aged 12) and Helen (aged 5) were scholars, and would later become school teachers. The fact that Sarah (aged 15) was also recorded as being a scholar, indicates that the Simpson family were better off than most working class Glaswegians.

After being brought up in privileged circumstances in Malaga, Sarah found it difficult to settle in Glasgow and longed to return to Spain. At the age of seventeen she ran away from home, breaking all ties with her family. Sarah travelled to Leith, some 50 miles away, where she found a job as a cook and then as a ship's stewardess. Women were employed on passenger vessels because the owners saw the benefit of hiring them, especially as stewardesses to care for their female customers and children. The young Sarah became pregnant and on 31st July 1873 she gave birth to an illegitimate son Alfred Simpson at the Royal Maternity Hospital in Edinburgh. Presumably friends looked after Alfred since Sarah later went to work for the London & Edinburgh Shipping Company, where she met Robert Kirkpatrick for the very first time. Official Crew Agreements for the SS Iona reveal that in 1879, Robert (aged 41) held the position of First Mate, while Sarah (aged 24) was employed as a stewardess. The couple entered into a clandestine relationship and the married Robert began to lead a double life. Sarah became pregnant and on 2nd July 1880 she gave birth to another son James at 5 Pattison Street, Leith. Since Robert was married his name was not recorded as the father and James Simpson was registered as being illegitimate.

One might think Robert Kirkpatrick justified his infidelity with the younger Sarah Simpson because he'd outgrown his wife Mary, the humble domestic servant. After all, he was on the verge of becoming a Master Mariner and Sarah was 'educated' and had a thirst for travel. However, Robert and Mary's marriage fell apart because of something far more serious. Many years later Sarah would tell her daughter Annie that Robert's 'first wife' was a drunkard and he finally decided to leave her when he found himself with his foot on her throat. On the point of disaster, he said "you're not worth it" and walked out on her.

In February 1881 Robert Kirkpatrick (aged 43) obtained his Certificate of Competency as a Master of a Home Passenger Ship. It must have been a proud moment for a self educated man who had been to sea for nearly 30 years. However, Robert wasn't qualified to skipper vessels overseas and this would limit his job prospects to the coastal trade. New commands were always in short supply and he didn't captain his first vessel for the London & Edinburgh Shipping Company, the SS Iona, until May.

The census returns of April 1881 indicate that by this time Robert's marriage had broken down. His wife Mary and their youngest son William (aged 7) were now living with her brother's family at Whitekirk in North Berwick where they were registered as 'borders', not as 'visitors'. Andrew Kirkpatrick, Mary's second oldest son (aged 16), does not show up on the census; while her eldest son Robert (aged 19) was working as an engine fitter in Kirkcaldy, Fife. Sarah Simpson was still living at Pattison Street with her two sons (Alfred, aged 7 years old and James aged, 9 months). At this time she was working in a factory as a flax dresser, a person who carries out the early stages of preparing flax for spinning to make linen. Robert Kirkpatrick was recorded as being 1st Mate onboard the SS Marmion off the Firth of Forth. Although Robert had left his wife, he didn't abandon his family. It would appear that he remained on good terms with his son Robert (known as Bob) and sent money to help support his son William, without Mary's knowledge.

On 2nd February 1882 Sarah gave birth to a girl, named Maggie Low Kirkpatrick Simpson, at 5 Largo Place, Leith.

Robert's mother's maiden name was Margaret Low. Sarah registered the birth and stated her occupation as a stewardess. Again, Robert was not recorded as being the father and Maggie was registered as being illegitimate. Sarah affectionately referred to her daughter as Marguerite, most probably, because it was the name of a friend, teacher or servant during her childhood in Malaga. In December 1884 Sarah gave birth to a second girl who was named Sarah Simpson Kirkpatrick by her parents, who registered the birth together. By this time the couple were living in Allan Street and Sarah stated her occupation as a factory worker. It's interesting to note that Robert gave his surname to his daughter, but because the couple weren't married she was recorded as being illegitimate.

The New Year turned out to be anything but happy for Robert and Sarah. Tragically, their son James and daughter Sarah both died of scarlet fever; a bacterial infection of the throat which claimed the lives of many children in this pre-antibiotic era. On 1st July 1885 James Simpson died after a six day illness at Allan Street. Sarah registered the death the next day, on what would have been James' 5th birthday. The couples' baby girl Sarah (aged 6 months) also contracted the disease and died on 10th July, after a seven day illness. With Robert away at sea this must have been a traumatic time for Sarah and no doubt she feared the worst for her son Alfred and daughter Maggie. Strangely enough Sarah's first born child Alfred does not appear on any official records after the 1881 census, either in Scotland or England. There's no record of his death in 1885, so he didn't die of scarlet fever along with James and Sarah. One possible explanation is that he was sent away from the family home to prevent him catching the highly contagious disease. If this was the case, somehow Alfred (aged 11) became estranged from his parents. Thankfully, the couples' daughter Maggie survived the ordeal.

In March 1886 Robert's time with the London & Edinburgh Shipping Company came to an abrupt end and he received the following reference:-

Dear Sirs

This is to certify that the bearer Mr. Robert Kirkpatrick has served in this company's service as master and mate for the last nine years, is sober and attentive to his duties. We dispensed with his service on account of his ship being laid up.

Thomas Aitken

(Manager)

Official records show that the company's vessels were regularly 'laid up' for repairs, for as long as three months. The termination of Robert's employment may have acted as a catalyst for him to leave his home town of Leith. Many years later Sarah told her daughter Annie that Robert had taken her to Spain. This trip abroad, most probably to Malaga, took place after he'd been laid off. In all likelihood Robert worked his passage on a ship bound for Malaga or a nearby port, while Sarah and their daughter Maggie were fee paying passengers. If Alfred Simpson was with the family it's possible that he died abroad, hence the lack of a death certificate in Scotland or England. After spending some time in Malaga, Sarah once again became pregnant. The prospect of returning to Leith, where her son and daughter had died, filled Sarah with dread.

Instead, the couple decided to start a new life in the North East of England. Their destination was Tyne Dock in South Shields, a place Robert was familiar with.

THREE

TYNE DOCK, SOUTH SHIELDS

South Shields is situated in a peninsula setting where the River Tyne meets the North Sea. It has about six miles of river frontage and three miles of coastline. Throughout the nineteenth century the river was dredged to stop sand accumulating at its entrance and making it hazardous for bigger vessels to enter. The mouth of the river was exposed to the full force of the sea and numerous ships were wrecked during bad weather with the loss of many lives. To overcome these problems two piers were built either side of the river: one at South Shields, County Durham and the other at Tynemouth in the county of Northumberland. Work began in 1854 and although the piers weren't fully completed until 1895, even the partly completed structures proved to be a success.

The late nineteenth century saw a dramatic increase in the population of South Shields, the proportional increase in the 1880's being the highest in England. The population rose from 35,239 in 1861 to 56,875 in 1881 and 92,263 in 1901. The town grew as a result of the success of the mining and ship building industries on Tyneside, which led to the construction of a huge coal-shipping dock. The work was originally undertaken by the 'Railway King' George Hudson when he was chairman of the York, Newcastle & Berwick Railway Company. Over 130 acres of waste land on the western border of South Shields with the neighbouring town of Jarrow, was purchased from the church authorities. Work commenced in 1849, but within ten months the excavations were suspended because of lack of money. It wasn't until 1856 with the formation of the North Eastern Railway Company that work began again by the new owners, who completed the construction of the dock within three years. The railway company also built houses for its employees, a few hundred yards from the dock. These included the aptly named Dock Street and Bede Street, as well as Lord Nelson, Whitehead and Hudson Street. The dock and surrounding area would eventually become part of the newly created Tyne Dock municipal ward of South Shields. The residents of this working class part of the town were mainly dock workers, railway men and seamen. Soon the population would exceed 5,000 with people coming from all over the British Isles, as well as Scandinavia and the Baltic ports, to settle in the area.

The water area of the original dock comprised 50 acres with the depth of water being 24ft at an average spring tide. Vessels were admitted by a tidal lock, 100ft wide by 250ft in length, through a main entrance gate 80ft in width. The dock was capable of taking 400 to 500 small sailing ships known as collier brigs, which were designed for carrying coal. Railway lines ran along the top of 4 wooden staithes from the river bank and rose at a gradient, enabling locomotives to shunt coal wagons to an appropriate height for loading colliers anchored alongside. The 4 staithes each had 5 coal-spouts on each side enabling 40 colliers to be loaded at the same time. The success of the dock was guaranteed with the development of a fleet of steam powered colliers at Palmer's shipyard in Jarrow. These revolutionary vessels were capable of carrying 650 tons of coal to London and returning in a week, when previously it had taken sailing ships between 2 to 4 weeks depending upon the weather. The railway company provided the coal owners of Durham (the biggest producers in the world) with a cost-effective solution of transporting their coal via Tyne Dock staithes to London and the rest of the world. The ties between the capital and South Shields were very strong and the town borrowed many of its riverside street names from London including Holborn and Wapping Street. It was said that Shields collier crews knew the contours of the Thames almost as well as they did the Tyne.

The growth of the mining and shipbuilding industries on Tyneside gave rise to a great increase in the consumption of timber and the dock was set out to handle this 'hungry cargo'. In 1892 some £80,000 was spent on new coal staithes, and another £90,000 on deepening and widening the entrance to the dock for larger steam ships. By now the dock was handling other traffic and the facilities included large wharehouses for the storage of grain. Nevertheless, coal remained the principal cargo and the tonnage shipped increased from nearly 1,500,000 tons in 1860 to just over 7,000,000 tons in 1902. The river was packed with vessels and a forest of funnels and masts pierced the Tyne Dock skyline, from whose staithes more coal was transported than from any coal-shipping dock in the world. If the truth be told, the expression "carrying coals to Newcastle" (to describe a pointless activity) could more accurately have been "carrying coals to South Shields". Ironically the town's St. Hilda Colliery used their own established Harton staithes, rather than those of the magnificent Tyne Dock.

Tragically, the town's development into a busy port made it vulnerable to disease and there were two cholera fatalities as late as 1893. More serious, was the smallpox epidemic of 1870-71 which affected 4,000 people - one in ten of the population - of whom 373 died. Precautions were so lax that a seaman was allowed to come ashore, in so advanced a stage of smallpox that he died in the waiting room at Tyne Dock Railway Station, despite his captain having declared that there was no sickness aboard his ship. It was this epidemic that led the town to create a proper Sanitary Department and appoint a Medical Officer in 1874, long after most towns had taken this step. Precautions began to be taken regarding incoming ships and a floating 'quarantine hospital' was constructed further along the river, near to the town's Customs House at Mill Dam.

Shields' greater importance and size (it covered 4,300 acres and had a population of 90,000) reflected in its attaining County Borough status in 1889. One of the first duties was to commence the opening of three new public parks at the coast, which were largely levelled from old ballast hills at the mouth of the river. However, the town's true coming of age began in 1896 with the South Shields Corporation Act, which authorised many improvements over the next decade. These included the widening of major roads; the introduction of an electrical tramway service; the construction of quayside buildings and slaughterhouses; the development of recreational facilities at the seaside and the clearance of slums at the riverside dating back to the eighteenth century.

FOUR

THE KIRKPATRICK FAMILY

In the autumn of 1886 Robert Kirkpatrick brought the pregnant Sarah Simpson and their daughter Maggie to Tyne Dock. After spending several months in Spain the couple had very little money to their name. They set up home as 'Mr. and Mrs. Kirkpatrick' at 47 Bede Street, close to the Tyne Dock arches over which the railway lines ran to the staithes. In spite of being a Master Mariner new commands were always in short supply and Robert would not skipper a ship for the rest of his working life. Records show that by October 1886 he was working as a Chief Mate on the SS Julia Wiener (tonnage 627); 'carrying coals' to his home town of Leith, Cardiff and abroad. In January 1887, while Robert was at sea, Sarah gave birth to another daughter and named her Sarah.

By July 1887 Robert had joined the crew of the SS South Moor (tonnage 972). She was a London owned collier (built by Palmer's of Jarrow) who mainly plied her trade between the north east coast and the capital. With vessels arriving at the Thames at all hours of the day and night, transporting coal to the world's busiest river was a hazardous task. On Wednesday afternoon 22nd August 1888 the South Moor left Tyne Dock with a cargo of coal for London. As she was proceeding up the Thames at 3.30am on Friday morning a Hartlepool steamer, the Winston, struck her with a tremendous blow on the starboard side and the South Moor began to sink. Robert and the rest of the crew had a very narrow escape. Some of them had just enough time to take to the deck and were rescued by a passing boat, while others succeeded in scrambling onboard the colliding vessel. Fortunately, the South Moor was made of sturdy stuff; she was refloated and Robert worked on her as a 1st or 2nd Mate for nearly a decade.

In November 1888 Sarah gave birth to a third girl, Martha, affectionately known as Mattie. By 1890 the family were living in a three room terraced house at 10 Lee Street, soon to be renamed South Eldon Street. Their new home was situated only a few hundred yards from St. Mary's Church (C of E), Tyne Dock. At the rear of the house there was a backyard with an outside toilet which they shared with their nextdoor neighbours. An outer door led to a back lane which ran the length of the opposing houses in South Palmerston Street. There was no garden, the Kirkpatrick's front door opened onto the pavement and horse driven trams passed along the cobbled road on their way to the town's Market Place. On 7th March 1890 Sarah gave birth to a boy named James, who was known as Jamie by his 'Scottish parents'.

The 1891 Census reveals that Sarah had help looking after her four children provided by a 15 year old live-in domestic servant called Ettie Crozier. Robert had a steady job as a Chief Mate and the Kirkpatrick's were quite comfortable compared to their neighbours. It was into this environment that John (known as Jack) was born on the 6th July 1892 at 10 South Eldon Street. In November 1894, the family would be complete with the birth of Jack's sister Annie. Many years later she would say, "My brother and I were the two youngest and grew up very attached to one another. As a child his hair was fairish but as he grew older it darkened and he had very blue eyes."

Tragically, in December 1894, Jack's brother Jamie died (aged 4) another victim of scarlet fever. Robert was at home at the time and registered his death as 'James Kirkpatrick Simpson, son of Sarah Simpson (of no occupation)'. The following death notice appeared in the town's evening newspaper, the Shields Daily Gazette & Shipping Telegraph, known locally as *The Gazette*.

> At 10 South Eldon Street on the 10th inst., Jamie, the dearly beloved son of Robert Kirkpatrick. To be interred at Harton New Cemetery on Thursday, December 13th, 1894.

The Kirkpatrick's may have been better off than most of their neighbours but with five children to provide for and given the need for secrecy, Jamie was buried in an unmarked grave without a headstone. Not surprisingly, Jack was incredibly special to his mother. She had lost three boys and had a dread of losing him.

Sadly, not all the children in and around the Tyne Dock area had such loving parents. When Jack was a baby, his sister Maggie brought a scruffy looking eight year old boy into the family home at South Eldon Street. He had no shoes or socks, was extremely dirty and complained of being hungry. Jack's mother took pity on the boy and gave him something to eat, and for a month he came nearly every day for meals. One day his nose was bleeding and he told Jack's mother his father had hit him. Later, a policeman found him crying in the street and unable to walk properly because of a sore on his foot. After making enquires the policeman took statements from Jack's mother and a number of ladies in the neighbourhood, who had seen him wandering the streets. The police visited the boys' house in Brunswick Street and subsequently his father appeared in court charged with unlawfully neglecting his child. It transpired that the boys' mother was in an asylum and after drinking heavily his father would beat him. The man was sentenced to two years in jail and the boy was taken into care.

During the first twelve years of Jack's life the Kirkpatrick family lived at five different addresses: 10 South Eldon Street (1892-1896), 119 Corbridge Street (1896-1897), 130 Frederick Street (1897-1898), 360 John Williamson Street (1899-1900) and 141 South Frederick Street (1900-1904). All of these properties were owned by private landlords and the streets were made up of rows of terraced houses separated by back lanes. Since the family were always on the move, one might think they had difficulty paying the rent. However, this was not the case because all of the changes of address were to properties with higher rents. The Kirkpatrick's weren't leaving a house secretly at night to avoid paying their rent (or as a Geordie would say, "doing a moonlight flit") - it was the opposite. If a better property was vacated the rent collector approached Jack's mother and asked if she was interested in taking it, knowing she could afford to pay the higher rent. Such 'moves', often to a house with an extra room or larger backyard, were a common occurrence at this time. Most people had very few possessions and they could easily be transported by hiring a cart or by paying a cartman to move larger items of furniture.

The houses of John Williamson Street (the longest street in the town) were built in the 1870's/1880's. They shared a back lane which stretched the length of both Frederick Street and South Frederick Street, a distance of three quarters of a mile. Most of these properties were in the neighbouring council wards of Rekendyke or Deans. They were sought after by the residents of the older houses of Tyne Dock since they had their own backyards and were further away from the noise of the railway wagons and the coal dust of the staithes. By 1900, Jack's father had been in steady employment for 13 years and the Kirkpatrick's were living at 141 South Frederick Street. Not only did they have their own backyard, but the front door opened onto a few descending steps to the pavement outside and there was a small wall at the front of the house. The Kirkpatrick's new home was situated only a few hundred yards away from St. Jude's Church (C of E). It was built in 1888 to cope with the massive influx of people into Tyne Dock and the surrounding area.

Robert Kirkpatrick was able to spend time with his family because of the watch-on-board and watch-ashore system operated by colliers. A system whereby half of the crew stayed on board attending to the loading/unloading whilst the other half went home. The next trip the watches changed over letting the first crew to have a spell at home and the other watch then looked after the loading/unloading. In common with other seafaring parents Robert would regale his children with stories of his adventures at sea. One that Maggie would tell her own children reflected her father's skill as a navigator. During stormy weather and without the aid of a pilot, he safely guided vessels into both Shanghai Harbour and Moreton Bay in Queensland.   Also, Annie would recall that her father was shipwrecked three times.   Other stories told by Robert include his near escape on the South Moor when 'carrying coals' to London and the time he left his ship in Australia to join a gold rush.

Like many seafarers Robert had a Life Insurance Policy with his supposed wife 'Sarah Kirkpatrick' being the beneficiary. In view of his real wife's drinking problem, Robert and Sarah may have thought she wouldn't live long and then they could finally be married. However, much to her credit Mary mended her ways and gave up the demon drink. She became a doting grandmother to her son Bob's children and outlived her husband by nearly 19 years.

FIVE

BARNES ROAD SCHOOL

Jack began his education at the local Barnes Road School, situated on the corner of South Palmerston Street and Barnes Road. Converted from a disused railway station in 1849 it was originally a school for the children of the workmen of the nearby Jarrow Chemical Works. The buildings had also been used as a temporary church by local people prior to the building of St. Mary's Church (C of E), Tyne Dock in 1862. The school's first headmaster was known to his pupils as Mr. Fraser. By a strange coincidence he left Shields for Australia and later became the Reverend Duncan Fraser of Heidelberg, Melbourne. The Barnes Road Mixed Infants School opened in 1863 and by this time children from the local neighbourhood were also in attendance. In 1883 the entire school was handed over to South Shields School Board who implemented a range of improvements. The buildings were enlarged to include a separate Junior School with Boys and Girls Departments, which catered for children up to age eleven. The entire school was known locally as 'The Barnes'.

Jack's parents must have thought that education was important since on the 14th October 1895 *'John Kirkpatrick'* was admitted to the Infants, aged 3 years and 3 months. He was accompanied to school by his older sister Martha, aged 7, who was in attendance at the Junior Girls Department. School records show that Jack temporarily left the Infants after only four months, as he was deemed to be 'too young'. In September 1896 he was re-admitted, aged 4 years and 2 months, along with 262 children from Tyne Dock and the neighbouring area. The headmistress of the Infants was Miss Tulloch and one of Jack's teachers was a pupil teacher Miss Mary Ann Robertson, who also taught his sister Martha. Pupil teachers tended to be bright children who remained at school after the school leaving age to train as teachers.

The children sat at double desks made of heavy wood and wrought iron, built for longevity rather than comfort. The teacher's desk stood on a raised platform, so that mischief could easily be detected. Jack and his schoolmates were introduced to the three R's: Reading, wRiting and aRithmetic. The whole class would recite sentences such as 'the cat sat on the mat' and the 'two times' table and so on. Although most of the lessons followed the same pattern of rote learning and repetition, the children also had a weekly Object Lesson. Teachers were supplied with a variety of carved wooden animals, household items and clothing materials, and the infants were given a chance to learn by using their own personal observations.

As books and paper were expensive, the children wrote on slates using a sharpened piece of slate known as a slate pencil. Many of the girls hung a little cloth bag around their neck in which they kept a damp rag to clean their slates, whereas the boys invariably used the sleeve of their pullovers or 'gansies' as the locals called them. At this time corporal punishment was the order of the day and pupils were caned if they stepped out of line. According to one teacher, "The young children were very muted and one had to draw replies from them, as blood from a stone." However, the infants found their voices during playtime, as the following entry in the Junior School log book reveals:

> Owing to the noise made by the infants at play, I'm compelled to change the Reading Session of Standard I from morning 11.00 to 12.00 and of Standard III to afternoon 3.45 to 4.30.

On 3rd July 1899, a few days short of his 7th birthday, *'John Kirkpatrick'* was admitted to Barnes Road Junior School along with 97 pupils from the Infants. The girls were housed on the ground floor and the boys were upstairs; neither met, not even in the playgrounds which were separate. Jack stayed at the Boys Department for the next four years (in standard I, IIa, III and IV) until June 1903. His friends at 'The Barnes' included William Voyce (b. 1890), Henry George (b. 1890) and Wilfred Robson (b. 1891). In common with the Kirkpatrick family, the Robson's used to live in Corbridge Street prior to moving to South Frederick Street. As a child growing up with Scottish parents, Jack's Geordie accent had a Scottish brogue which didn't go amiss with his classmates. Many years later Wilf Robson recalled that he'd been friends with the young Kirkpatrick from the age of eight and some of the boys had called him Jock.

In addition to taking the Barnes Infants, the Juniors also admitted pupils from neighbouring infant schools in South Shields and Jarrow. By August 1899 there were 502 boys at the school and the headmaster Joseph Willis wrote the following entry in the log book:

At the Managers meeting it was proposed that no more boys be admitted to the school except in exceptional cases.

Unfortunately, the proposal wasn't adhered to and on average there were 600 boys at the school. Not surprisingly, conditions were cramped and over the years Jack found himself in a class of 50-60 boys. Together with the Junior Girls and the Infants, the total number of pupils at 'The Barnes' in 1901 was 1,413.

The school curriculum for the Boys Department included Dictation, Grammar, Composition, Geography, Arithmetic, Algebra and Scripture. As the children grew older they would write in a lined book, using a dip pen and ink from out of an inkwell. Pupils would practice their handwriting by copying from the blackboard, until the entire page was full of identical lines. If an ink pen leaked it caused smears and the children were punished for 'blotting their copybooks'. All classes were routinely tested and any boy deemed to be 'slow' would not advance to the next year, but remained in his standard for another year. It wasn't all work and no play, since a young teacher called Jonathan Deaton organized the boys into football teams during playtime.

On 18th May 1900 the school was decorated with flags by the children in anticipation of the Relief of Mafeking during the Boer War. For nearly seven months a British garrison commanded by Colonel Baden-Powell were surrounded by a large Boer force, who continually shelled the town and tried to starve them into surrendering. British reinforcements finally broke through the Boer lines and Baden-Powell was the hero of the hour. The news was greeted with hysterical rejoicing throughout the country including South Shields where crowds sang, danced and cheered themselves hoarse. On 21st May the children of Barnes Road School took part in the town's celebrations. Jack and the rest of the boys were marched in procession, accompanied by a band, to some open ground off Ogle Terrace where they congregated for the singing of patriotic songs. The school log book also reveals that on 3rd July 1902 there was a day without lessons as part of the Coronation Festivities for Edward VII. The children engaged in sports in the schoolyard, after which tea and cakes were distributed. This was followed by a minstrel entertainer, then the children were given a bag of sweets and dismissed for the day.

The amount of money 'The Barnes' received from the School Board was dependant on the number of pupils at the school with an additional grant for good attendance. In order to encourage children to come to school, prize giving books were awarded annually in all classes for high attendance. These were much sought after since most parents couldn't afford to buy books for their children. Jack's attendance was excellent and school records reveal that over a three year period (1899 - 1902) he was only absent for two days. In his final year his attendance was again exemplary and in the summer of 1903 he was awarded a prize giving book 'for regular and punctual attendance and good behaviour'. Jack's book was a seafaring adventure entitled 'The Brig and the Lugger' by Hugh Mulleneaux Walmsley. Set in the aftermath of the French Revolution and during the Napoleonic Wars, the novel was a common prize giving book for schools. Thankfully, this hardback book has withstood the test of time and its red outer cover and all of the pages are in excellent condition. The inscription inside reads: *'Awarded to John Kirkpatrick'* and it's signed by Walton Smith of Barnes Road School. The book contains four black & white plates; two of them featuring sailing ships and is over 200 pages long. One can't help but speculate whether this book influenced his own decision to go to sea. Jack's attendance record reflects well on his parents and their relative financial position compared with other families in the neighbourhood. At the beginning of the twentieth century many working class parents didn't see the point of educating their children and some (especially girls) were kept off school to look after their younger siblings.

Jack's attendance record may have been exemplary but the same could not be said for his behaviour. On the 15th February 1900, Mr. Willis received a punishment book from the School Board. It was habitually maintained in respect of the various offences committed by the children such as disobedience, talking in class, rudeness or fighting. The book reveals that during Jack's time at Barnes Road School he was caned on six separate occasions for being surly. In Victorian/ Edwardian England surliness was associated with arrogance, a trait disliked by teachers who saw it as an affront to their authority. It's possible that Jack's better than average financial status gave him a demeanor, which was disapproved of by some of his teachers.

The fact that Jack was rarely absent from school indicates that he enjoyed good health. However, this was not the case for many of the children at 'The Barnes'. The school log book for October 1900 reveals that 38 boys were absent in one week due to 'infectious diseases'. Although measles was the most common cause of absenteeism more serious diseases claimed the lives of many children, particularly girls. On 20th April 1899, Jack's sister '*Martha Kirkpatrick*', aged 10, was removed from the Girls Department with 'a diseased hip'. Hip joint disease (or tuberculosis of the hip) was not uncommon in South Shields at this time and there was no known cure. In child sufferers there may be no complaint of pain during the day, but Jack's mother probably heard Martha cry out in her sleep at night. These are the so-called 'night cries' and are due to the decrease of voluntary muscle tone when a child goes to sleep, permitting the painful joint to be moved more when the child is asleep. As the disease developes swelling and limitation of motion maybe noted by the sufferer; followed by loss of weight, fatigue and general debility in the advanced stages of the disease.

Tragically, on 22nd October 1900, Martha died. Three days later Robert Kirkpatrick registered her death under the name '*Martha Simpson*', while a death notice published in *The Gazette* read as follows:-

KIRKPATRICK. At 141 So. Frederick Street on the 22nd inst. Martha (Mattie) the dearly beloved daughter of Robert and Sarah Kirkpatrick aged 11 years and 11 months. To be interred at Harton Cemetery on Saturday at 2.30pm. All friends please accept this (the only) intimation.

On hearing the sad news Miss Winter, Headmistress of the Girls Department, wrote the following entry in the school log book:

Martha Kirkpatrick, a late pupil of this school died on Monday after a very long and painful illness.

Martha's funeral took place on Saturday 27th October and the minister present was the Reverend Majendie of St. Jude's Church. The service took place in the chapel at Harton Cemetery, which was the tradition at the time. Another indication of the family's improving financial situation can be gauged by the fact that Robert Kirkpatrick purchased a funeral plot for three people; presumably thinking ahead to the time when he and Sarah would be buried with Martha, and this would prove to be the case.

SIX

PEGGIE AND WILL

In September 1900 Jack's sister Maggie (aged 18 and now known as Peggie) married William Thompson Balneaves. The 23 year old Will was living in the neighbouring town of Sunderland and had recently qualified as a photographer. The marriage took place at St. Michael's & The Angels, the Parish Church of Hendon, Bishopwearmouth. Initially, the couple lived with Will's parents at 7 Ann Street in Sunderland. Will and his siblings were born in Aberdeen and their father John Balneaves (a cashier) had brought them to the boom area of the North East of England.

The couple met in the late 1890's when Will was apprenticed to James Downey and Sons, a photographer's of 17 & 19 Eldon Street. The latter was a continuation of South Eldon Street but was situated in the neighbouring council ward of Rekendyke. Many of the properties in Eldon Street were converted into businesses since they were close to Frederick Street, the main shopping area for the growing population of the west end of the town. Will's job as a fledgling photographer carried a certain status but didn't necessarily pay good money. Nevertheless, he went to work in a suit and aspired to having his own studio one day. Jack's mother and father were happy with Peggies choice of a husband, and no doubt Will's parents were pleased their son had married the daughter of a Master Mariner.

In 1855 William Downey set up the town's first photographic studio with his brothers Daniel and James, in a wooden building next to St. Hilda's Church at the Market Place. The business flourished as Victorians embraced the new technological wonder of the day and well-to-do local people rushed to have their photograph taken for the very first time. Robert Ingham, the Member of Parliament for South Shields sat for the Downey brothers as did most of the town's Mayors, business fraternity and clergy. Branches were later opened north of the river at Newcastle, Morpeth and Blyth in Northumberland, and soon the brothers reputation grew far beyond the North East.

In January 1862 Downey's received a Royal Order from Queen Victoria for photographs of the Hartley Colliery Disaster which had gripped the whole nation. The mining accident (near Blyth) entombed 204 men and boys who could not be rescued, and so suffocated and died. Shortly afterwards William and Daniel Downey moved to London and established a studio at 5 Eaton Street. Over the years they produced portraits of most of the countries leading parliamentarians including Disraeli, Gladstone and Lord Palmerston. Their first royal photograph was of the Princess of Wales (later Queen Alexandria) taken at York Agricultural show in 1865. William Downey was shortly after commanded to photograph the Prince of Wales (later King Edward VII) and subsequently to make the first of many pictures of Queen Victoria. The Downey's received a Royal Warrant in 1879 and William Downey went on to earn the title of the Queen's Photographer. It wasn't long before the press of the day reported:

Mr. W. Downey has photographed nearly every living crowned head of Europe, as well as two Emperors of Russia and three Sultans of Turkey.

By the 1890's James Downey's studio at Eldon Street advertised the following range of photographic services: pictures of all kinds carefully copied, portraits reduced to fit lockets or enlarged to life size, special facilities for outdoor photography and negatives for future copies. In 1897 William Downey's son, a partner in the associated firm of J. & F. Downey of South Shields received a command to go to Balmoral to photograph Queen Victoria and her family for Her Majesties Diamond Jubilee. Will Balneaves was among a number of photographic assistants who were accommodated in the labourers cottages on the Balmoral Estate for the royal shoot. The young Will came away with a souvenir of the trip which he treasured for the rest of his life (and is still in the possession of the Balneaves family); a piece of tartan cloth used as a backdrop for a photograph of Queen Victoria. Under the tutorage of the Downey family Will became a skilled photographer and developed a knack for taking self portraits. He took the only surviving photograph of himself and Peggie in Shields by using a stand-in, before moving into place and taking the shot with a long release cord.

On 28th May 1901 Peggie gave birth to her first child, Martha Jane. She was born at Ann Street in Sunderland and named after Peggies recently departed sister. By the following year the Balneaves' had moved in with the Kirkpatrick's at South Frederick Street. On 10th November 1902 Peggie gave birth to her second child, John Robert. In order to distinguish him from his uncle John and his grandfather Robert, he became known as Bob. Finally, in May of 1905, Peggie gave birth to the baby of the family George. By now the Balneaves' were living in Newcastle, where Will was employed as a photographic assistant at Taylor's studios. Apparently, Will could earn more as an assistant photographer at Taylor's of Newcastle than he could as a photographer at Downey's, hence with a young family to think of he followed the money.

Over the years Will was responsible for most of the photographs of the Kirkpatrick family including the only surviving one of Jack as a child. It shows a smart looking boy with a carnation in his jacket lapel and, once again, illustrates the relatively comfortable life style of the Kirkpatrick's. The photograph was most probably taken at the christening of Bob or George Balneaves, when Jack was between 10 and 12 years old. Both Bob and George inherited their father's prominent ears and being 'Sons of the North East' they were keen footballers. Jack and his sister Annie were close to their nephews and niece. Many years later George Balneaves would refer to Annie as his favourite aunt when growing up on Tyneside.

SEVEN

MURPHY'S FAIR
AND
THE DONKEY BOY

In the late 1800's and early 1900's a travelling show family called Murphy held a fair at the town's Market Place. A private Act of Parliament which enabled the Market Square to be laid out ensured the townsfolk had permission to hold a fortnightly fair, twice a year.   Anticipating a high rate of truancy, the School Board wisely gave two half day holidays in May and November when the fair rolled into town. Murphy's Fair was a magnet for the town's children including Jack and a playmate from John Williamson Street called Billy Lowes. Many years later he would recall that Jack always found something to do amongst the roundabouts and the sideshows of Murphy's Fair. Billy Lowes (b. 1888) first met Jack when the Kirkpatrick family were living at 141 South Frederick Street (1900-1904). At this time Billy used to go with his mother to visit his grandmother Mrs. Mary Lillie, who lived only a few doors away from the Kirkpatrick's.   Although Billy was four years older than Jack he was small for his age and the two boys played together.   Both had a mutual interest: they kept pet rabbits in their backyards. Billy had Flemish Giants, while Jack preferred Belgian Giants, and sometimes they swapped their pets.

At the beginning of the twentieth century the Market Place, with the Town Hall at its centre, was the focal point of South Shields. Horse drawn trams arrived from Tyne Dock, travelled along the busy shopping areas of King Street and Ocean Road to the coast and back again. The children of Tyne Dock could not afford to travel by tram and would walk the few miles to play at Murphy's Fair. The nearer they got the more the excitement would build, especially on hearing the sound of the hurdy gurdy music and the tired legs of the smaller children found a spring in their step as the music kept calling them. Before long they could smell the fish stalls mingled with the sweetness of roasted nuts and the unmistakable aroma of horse manure. Finally, they found themselves confronted by the canopies of the roundabouts, a helter skelter constructed around a wooden lighthouse and a whole host of sideshows.

Children and adults alike queued for a puppet 'peep-show', consisting of a large box you peered into to watch moving puppets re-enact historical events. At this time the most popular shows featured the Funeral of William IV and the Coronation of Queen Victoria. Among the many strange attractions were a muscle man demonstrating various feats of strength; a quack doctor who sold the 'Elixir of Life' which cured all ills from the common cold to baldness; a man who removed cataracts with a knife and if you wished to be weighed there was a huge pair of scales with a chair suspended and balanced with various weights. The proprietors offer was, "If I cannot judge your weight within three pounds I shall not charge you anything, but if I am successful it will cost you three-pence."

All sorts of treats were on offer for the hungry crowds at the fair courtesy of muffin sellers, ginger bread makers and piemen. The latter sold a variety of pies, which according to mischievous boys contained dubious fillings such as cats and dogs. A number of highly coloured beverages were also advertised for sale, as refreshing 'cooling drinks'. Then, of course, there was the children's favourite the sweet sellers. Jack and his friends gazed upon stall holders making sweets using a large brass pan standing on a spirit stove. Into the pan was poured water and sugar with flavouring such as lemon and the mixture was brought to the boil. It was then poured out onto a marble slab and dusted over with icing sugar; folded, kneaded and rolled over like a huge sausage. This was then flung up into the air onto a large hook fastened to one of the stalls uprights and it was stretched out in a long ribbon; then laying it on a slab it was sliced into triangular pieces with a pair of cutters. These were called lemon clips and cost a penny a quarter and for variety the flavouring was changed using peppermint or ginger.

The most popular attraction for Jack and the rest of the children were Murphy's roundabouts. Under a garish striped canopy punters were spun around on 'galloping horses' to the sound of hurdy gurdy music, all powered by a giant steam engine. Walter Murphy and his wife Betsy created a travelling showman dynasty in the North of England with their three son's John (b.1855), William (b.1858) and Thomas (b. 1860). By the 1900's the roundabout in all its shapes and forms was becoming an established feature of any reputable fair. Roundabout owners developed innovative designs for their rides with eye catching names, such as Racing Cockerels and Proud Peacocks. The

Murphy family were no exception, as is evident from the following newspaper report in 1900:

> William Murphy's royal patent stud of Jumping Ostriches was having a fine time. Why the human being likes to be 'jumped' is one of those things difficult to understand but he does and Murphy was the people's jumper on Saturday.

Nevertheless, many Victorian's had to be reassured about the safety of roundabouts as they thought being spun around at high speeds was unnatural. To allay their fears roundabout canopies displayed captions such as 'Finest Invention and Safe Exercise', indicating that far from being a health hazard they were actually good for you.

Murphy's Fair would eventually become too big for the Market Place and over the years the town developed its own fair at the coast. John Murphy did lease 'the sands' from the council for a short period of time, but due to problems in transporting his roundabouts he pulled out of the venture. The Murphy brothers went on to become leading lights in the North Eastern Roundabout Proprietors Syndicate and regularly won the tender to supply the Newcastle Town Moor Fair, known as 'the Hoppings'. However, the memory of Murphy's Fair lingered on in South Shields and because of its bustling nature it gave rise to a colloquialism to describe a chaotic scene. Whether it be an untidy workplace or an unruly classroom of children, someone from the town can be heard to exclaim, "It's like Walter Murphy's Fair."

All of his life Jack loved animals and during the school summer holidays of 1902 he worked on the donkey rides at the town's seasonal fair at Herd Sand. The latter is believed to be a dialect corruption of Heord, an old English word meaning flock. The name Herd Sand preceded the building of the mile long South Pier which began in 1854. It was completed in 1895 and affectively cut Herd Sand into a little and big beach. The fair took place on the little beach which stretched from the groyne at the mouth of the river to the South Pier, a distance of a few hundred yards. The big beach stretched from the southern side of the pier, for nearly a mile, to a rocky headland known as Trow Rocks.

In its early days the fair at the coast was a makeshift event and had none of Murphy's revolutionary steam powered roundabouts. However, the beach was ideal for donkey rides, coconut shies and swing boats, or as the locals called them shuggy boats. These were an early type of fairground ride with a child sat either side of a carriage (or boat), suspended from an 'A' shaped wooden frame. The boats were made to swing back and forward by pulling on a rope threaded through an overhead pulley. A variety of stall holders sold refreshments, such as homemade lemonade and sweets for the children. Little girls would buy long strips of 'hanky panky toffee' about half an inch wide and hang it around their neck as decoration. One old lady had a stall with a spirit stove and sold hot water for people to make tea with, as they picnicked on the beach. A barrel organ would thump out a tune at the turn of a handle and to the amazement of the children, a monkey with a collecting tin would elicit donations.

Among the wooden cabins on Herd Sand were those belonging to the Johnson, Wilkie and Michelson families.

Jimmy Michelson, in partnership with James Howe Wilkie, hired boats for trips around the harbour and to the end of the pier where Michelson's mother ran a tea room. Over the years Jimmy took part in many rescues at sea, helping to launch boats and supporting the shore operations of the town's Volunteer Life Brigade. As long ago as 1890 the Michelson's constructed a wooden 'gravity ride' at Herd Sand, billed as their very own 'Patent Safety Switchback Railway'. Customers sat in an open carriage and were winched up an incline where they were released and left to free fall up and down an undulating track, the carriage returning to the start by its own momentum. At this time a switchback railway 'roller coaster' at Skegness, on the Lincolnshire coast, charged three-pence a ride and newspaper articles speculated as to its impact on the donkey trade.

Jack was ten years old when he worked on the donkey rides and according to his sister Annie, "he loved it". Her brother secured the much sought after position of a donkey boy through a school friend, Henry George of Florence Street. Each summer his father Joe, hired out several donkeys belonging to a local farmer. Joseph George (b.1864) was a coal miner by trade, who due to health problems gave up working down the pit and did a variety of jobs including selling fish 'door to door'. Mr. George (as he was known by his boys) was an animal lover and as a miner had worked with pit ponies. On 26th June 1902 he took part in the Coronation Day Horse Procession organized by the town council to celebrate the coronation of Edward VII. He entered a couple of his four legged friends in the Donkey Class, 'for those animals that have been regularly worked or let out for hire'.

The donkeys were tethered a short distance away from the stalls of the fair, next to Johnson's rowing boats which were for hire. Mr. George usually wore his Sunday best for work and was very particular when selecting his donkey boys. He invariably chose the cleanest and best dressed lads, since his customers tended to be the children of the more affluent townsfolk or visitors to South Shields. Like most donkey boys Jack wore a cloth cap, a waist length jacket and his trousers legs were tucked into his socks to avoid tripping over on the uneven surface. The donkey rides cost a penny and he was required to escort the donkey and its ride along the beach towards Herd Groyne and back again; prodding it with a cane stick to prompt its progress, if necessary. Jack's customers were usually smartly dressed children about his age or young ladies who rode side saddle. To cater for very small children Mr. George would place a specially constructed wicker basket saddle on the back of a donkey and the child's mother would accompany Jack as he slowly led the donkey on its journey along the beach. Many years later Jim Wilkinson (b. 1889), an old playmate from South Frederick Street, would recall that Jack gave many a child a free ride on a donkey. This was most probably said in jest, since Mr. George kept a watchful eye on his young charges. It was also customary for a donkey boy suspected of pocketing a fare to be held upside down and given a good shake to see if any coins fell to the ground.

Mr. George made sure his boys looked after their four legged workmates. Under his guidance Jack learnt the basics in handling a donkey including saddling and bridling. On a fine day he would work from 7.30 in the morning until 9 o'clock in the evening; during which time the donkeys had to be rested, watered and fed at intervals. At the end of each day Jack would help take the donkeys back to nearby stables and as a treat Mr. George allowed him to ride on one of them. For his labours Jack was paid the grand sum of sixpence a day and then he had to walk the two miles home. Little did anyone know the important part donkeys would play in his short life. According to Jack's nephew George Balneaves one of the donkeys at Herd Sand was called Murphy. At Gallipoli Jack used several donkeys and not surprisingly he christened one of them Murphy. Ironically, because of his Geordie accent, some Australian soldiers thought Jack was Irish and nicknamed him Murphy while others thought he was Scottish and dubbed him Scottie.

EIGHT

ST. MARY'S CHURCH

In common with many of the children from Barnes Road School, Jack attended St. Mary's Church (C of E), Tyne Dock. He was a member of the church's choir and its Sunday School. The church was situated in South Eldon Street, a few hundred yards from where Jack was born. It was built using some of the proceeds of the sale of the land by the church authorities for the construction of the Tyne Dock. The foundation stone was laid in 1861 by Robert Ingham MP and St. Mary's was consecrated the following year by the Bishop of Durham. The church was built by the esteemed architect John Dobson, who designed the magnificent Central Railway Station in Newcastle. The handsome gothic building consisted of a chancel, a knave of four bays, a vestry chamber, gallery and west porch.

St. Mary's could seat 646 people and was renowned for its prized Schulze organ - one of only three in the entire country. It was paid for by the wealthy businessman (and three times Mayor of South Shields) John Williamson, after whom the longest street in the town was named. The church's organist up until 1902 was William Rea M.A., who also taught singing at Barnes Road School. According to an ex-pupil, "The lessons usually ended by his rushing from the classroom with his hands covering his ears to shut out the painful discordance of the boys voices." By 1891 St. Mary's Parish contained 636 inhabited houses and a population of 5,703. Ten years later the number of inhabited houses had almost doubled to 1,173 and the population had increased to 10,300.

As long ago as 1851 it was agreed that a South Shields Sunday School Union should be formed in affiliation with the London Sunday School Union. The idea being to stimulate and encourage the teachers already engaged in the work of religious instruction, to establish Sunday Schools in every part of the town and to furnish them with libraries and teaching materials. A feature of the unions work was a Good Friday procession through the town of the Sunday School children. Although only the non-conformist churches 'marched' it became a big event in the town. By the turn of the twentieth century, thousands of people would gather at the Market Place in the culmination of the annual Procession of Witness. Church leaders would address the vast crowd from the steps of the Town Hall and the children were given an orange in a ceremony known as the Poor Christians Treat. Afterwards the crowds, all dressed in their Sunday best, would make their way to the coast. Brass bands played to huge audiences at the Marine Park, families took to the pier for a walk and the fair at Herd Sand was packed with visitors for most of the day.

In 1888 three out of four children in England and Wales attended Sunday School. Of these 2,200,000 belonged to the Church of England, and more than 3,000,000 were non-conformists. By 1900 there were 39 Sunday Schools in South Shields with a total of 8,758 scholars and 900 teachers, and the tradition of sending children to Sunday School had been firmly established. Since Robert and Sarah were not married and there is no record of their children being baptised, it's unlikely that the couple were churchgoers. However, it didn't stop them from sending their children to St. Mary's Church and the accompanying Sunday School, possibly to keep up appearances or simply to give themselves a break. The weekly Sunday School classes took place at St. Mary's Church Hall and were made up of boys and girls, aged between 6 and 14. By the time Jack and his sisters were in attendance St. Mary's Sunday School consisted of 'Bible Study, Scripture and the Singing of Hymns', through which the church spread its moral message to the working class children of Tyne Dock.

The first vicar of St. Mary's was the hard working James Jeremy Taylor, who served the people of Tyne Dock for over 30 years until his death in 1893. In his later years the Reverend Taylor suffered from ill-heath and was assisted in his duties by a young curate-in-charge George Lanchester King. The energetic Reverend King became the church's second vicar in 1894 and quickly set about spreading the word. Every week he gave an address to the workers in the dockyard and one of his talks was entitled, 'Why so many workman do not go to church?' During King's tenure the parish went from strength to strength and the church's Sunday School flourished. However, he left St. Mary's five years later to become the Bishop of Madagascar, a considerable achievement since he was only 38 years old. The Reverend King would later recall, "The parish of St. Mary's was delightfully friendly and full of loyal souls." In 1899, King was succeeded by the well respected Thomas Powell Williams (b.1857). He stayed until 1922 and was affectionately known by parishioners, in his latter years, as 'Daddy Williams'.

In 1904 St. Mary's vicarage was built off South Eldon Street on St. Mary's Terrace and T. P. Williams and his family were the first occupants. (Previous vicars had lived about a mile away at Simonside Lodge). Over the years he would be assisted in his duties by a number of curates including Morris Hodson and Clifford Barker. The Reverend Williams became a well known figure in the Tyne Dock area. He regularly visited Barnes Road School and routinely examined 'the Boys' (including Jack) in Scripture. As the vicar of St. Mary's he held the honorary position of Brother Chaplain of the Lord Barnard Lodge of Freemason's at Whitehead Street, Tyne Dock. Thomas Powell Williams was a relative of Baden-Powell and following the formation of the Scouts in 1908, St. Mary's developed a thriving scout troop. The latter included Robert Hogg (b. 1890) and Willie J. Bowman (b.1891), who both attended St. Mary's Sunday School with Jack. Willie lived in John Williamson Street and his Scottish father John Bowman, worked under Robert Kirkpatrick as a 2nd Mate onboard colliers. Many years later Willie would recall that he played cricket with Jack in the back lane using wickets chalked on a brick wall.

NINE

CHANGING FORTUNES

A few weeks short of his 11th birthday Jack left 'The Barnes' for Mortimer Road Senior School; a newly built three storey building situated off a residential street called Mortimer Road. The Mortimer Road Senior and Junior Mixed Board Schools were opened in August 1901 to cater for the ever growing population of the town. The Juniors occupied the ground floor and the Seniors the first floor, while on the second floor was a large gymnasium, joinery shop and cookery classroom. The Senior School was divided into Boys and Girls Departments; there were separate yards to play in and woe betide any boys found hanging around the girls playground. Both the Junior and Senior School could accommodate 600 pupils each, although when it opened there were only 800 children in total. A special feature of the new building was the combined ventilation and heating system. However, the latter wasn't a success since the school log book reveals that the council engineer was always being called out to repair it.

On 29th June 1903 *'John Kirkpatrick'* of 141 South Frederick Street was one of 128 boys to be admitted to Mortimer Road, as it was known locally. He enrolled alongside 27 of his classmates from Barnes Road School including Wilf Robson and William Voyce. Records show that his older Sunday School friends Willie Bowman and Robert Hogg were also at the school. The headmaster of the Senior School was John Wonders (nicknamed Johnny), while his counterpart at the Juniors was John Robertson (known as Robbie). Both were classmates as boys at 'The Barnes' in 1875, fellow teachers at South Shields High School and finally contemporaries as schoolmasters. They were also great friends and lived with their families in Stanhope Road, where many of the town's school teachers resided.

Jack's day began with assembly in the hall where the entire school would recite the Lord's Prayer. John Wonders was renowned for leading the singing; a particular favourite of his being the One Hundredth Psalm sung to a piano accompaniment. Mortimer Road was classed as an Elementary School and the teachers hoped to build on their pupils grasp of the three R's and introduce them to a range of academic subjects. The children were also instructed in practical activities, such as woodwork (for boys) and cookery (for girls), to equip them for adulthood and the world of work. The more academic pupils who passed examinations at '13 plus' were able to continue there education beyond their 14th birthday. However, the vast majority of the children left before then to take up jobs in local shipyards, engineering works and coal mines, to bring much needed money into the family home.

According to Annie her brother had little time for academic studies and was more prone to boyish pranks and escapades than school work. In fact his first heroic deed took place at one of his childhood haunts, the Tyne Dock Gut. The gut was a paved inlet sloping down to the river, constructed so that horses could back carts to the waters edge and load goods on and off barges. It was situated adjacent to Readhead's shipyard and prior to the construction of the Tyne Dock it was known locally as the Wesh-Shore, a dialect corruption of West Shore. Over the years it became a favourite play area for the children of Tyne Dock, especially at weekends and during the school holidays. Many of these children were too young to walk to Herd Sand, so they went paddling or crabbing at the gut. Young boys like Anthony Hails (b. 1896) of nearby H. S. Edwards Street would make rafts, while older lads would jump off a jetty and swim the short distance to the sloping inlet. One Saturday two children fell into the murky waters of the Tyne Dock Gut and seeing they were in trouble, Jack promptly jumped in and rescued them.

By the time Jack started school at Mortimer Road his father had been working on Fenwick's colliers for five years. Fenwick & Company was an old established Tyneside shipping company engaged in the Australian wool trade from 1834. In the mid-nineteenth century it moved into the coal trade with Stobart & Co., together with a subsidiary William France. In these early days its vessels ventured further afield to the Baltic ports and to Canada for the St. Lawrence coal trade. In 1901 John Fenwick & Son merged their business with those of William France, Stobart & Co. and H. C. Pelly to form France, Fenwick & Co. On its formation the new company was primarily involved with the coal trade from the north east of England to London and it would become one of the biggest collier owners in Britain.

Official Crew Agreements show that from 1898 to 1903 Robert worked onboard the Fenwick's collier SS Berrington (another vessel built at Palmer's shipyard). The river was a dangerous place to earn a living and collisions between vessels were common, as is evident from the following *Gazette* article, dated 24th March 1900.

> A serious accident occurred last night in Tyne Dock, while the screw collier Berrington was leaving for London, coal laden. The propeller of the Spanish steamer Miravilla penetrated the side of the Berrington causing a good size hole. Immediately the Berrington got clear she showed signs of sinking and great haste was made to get her out of the dock before she foundered. One of the dock tugs succeeded in getting the vessel into the basin, though not quite clear of the traffic, when she settled down. Extra assistance was given form the water boat and the steamers donkey engine was kept going through the night. Constant water pumping was carried on, while a diver was employed to secure the hole, so as to float the Berrington further towards the quay wall. This was done successfully and the vessel was moored. To keep the Berrington partially afloat the pumps have to be continuously kept going. The repairing of the damaged part will necessitate the discharge of part of the cargo. It is probable the Berrington will not be docked, but repaired afloat as the breach is only a little below the water level.

Luckily, Robert and the rest of the crew came through the ordeal unscathed. In addition to delivering coal to London, the Berrington also made frequent voyages to Rotterdam and the ports of Dieppe and St. Malo in France. On these trips Robert was away from home for several weeks at a time.

By January 1905 Robert Kirkpatrick was 67 years old and his seafaring days, which spanned some 50 years, were coming to an end. Contrary to popular belief, Robert's working career wasn't curtailed by an accident onboard a Fenwick's collier. Many years later Annie told her son that her father had suffered two strokes. Strokes occur due to problems with the blood supply to the brain and often lead to paralysis. It would appear that Robert suffered his first stroke at home, early in 1905. Sadly, there was no sickness benefits or old age pension at this time and the Kirkpatrick's better than average life style took a dramatic turn for the worse. In order to make ends meet Jack shared his bedroom with a number of lodgers and his mother had to 'take in washing'. His older sister Sarah (who is believed to have worked as a waitress) contributed a small amount to the household, but soon the family had to give up their home in South Frederick Street and find cheaper accommodation

The Kirkpatrick's eventually moved to 14 Bertram Street, a gable ended house on the corner of H. S. Edwards Street. Bertram Street was built on a slope, leading down towards the river. The family's new home was close to the main railway line into Shields and Readhead's shipyard. In the shadow of the shipyard Jack lived with the sounds of snapping ropes, droning drag chains and the vibrating clanging of steel upon steel. Bertram Street was a main thoroughfare for the engineering and shipyard workers of the Tyne. Outside the Kirkpatrick's front door the pavement reverberated to the sound of hobnail boots and people used to say, "you didn't need a knocker up if you lived in Bertram Street."

Jack's parents had hoped he would start work as an apprentice after leaving school with one of the many industrial firms in the town, such as Tyne Dock Engineering or Readhead's. However, according to Annie the wages of an apprentice were poor and the lack of money coming into the Kirkpatrick household put pay to that idea. Instead Jack left Mortimer Road School on the 23rd June 1905, two weeks short of his 13th birthday, to start work as a milkman. If Jack's prospects were on the wane, those of some of his classmates were heading upwards. William Voyce started work as an apprentice pattern maker, while Wilf Robson secured a position as an apprentice marine engineer. Initially their wages were poor but once qualified they would earn a lot more money than the unskilled Jack.

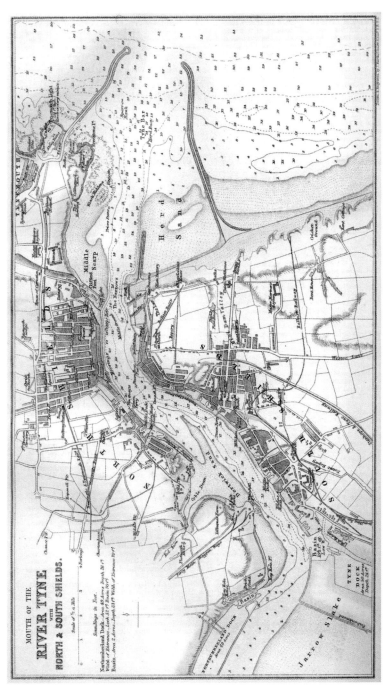

A map showing the Mouth of the River Tyne (circa. 1875).

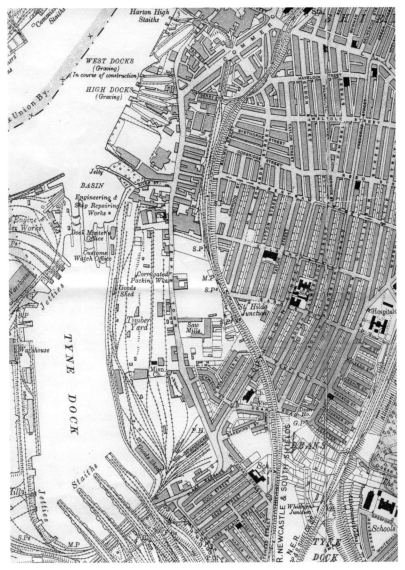

Tyne Dock and the surrounding streets (circa. 1900).

Tyne Dock Staithes after WW1.

South Eldon Street where Jack was born in 1892.

CN 405698

CERTIFIED COPY of an ENTRY OF BIRTH
Pursuant to the Births and Deaths Registration Act 1953

Registration District **South Shields**

1892 · Birth in the Sub-district of **Westoe** in the Counties of **South Shields and Durham**

No.	When and where born	Name, if any	Sex	Name and surname of father	Name, surname and maiden surname of mother	Occupation of father	Signature, description and residence of informant	When registered	Signature of registrar	Name entered after registration
Columns:-	1	2	3	4	5	6	7	8	9	10
223	Sixth July 1892 10 South Eldon Street Westoe USD.	John	Boy	Robert KIRKPATRICK	Sarah SIMPSON a Housekeeper (Domestic)	Seaman (Merchat Service)	Robert Kirkpatrick Father S. Simpson Mother 10 South Eldon Street Westoe	Third August 1892	James Sadwle	

Registrar.

NOTE: The 'Name, surname and maiden surname of mother' reads Sarah Simpson.

Annie (b. 1894)

Martha (b. 1888)

Sarah (b. 1887)

Peggie (b. 1882)

Barnes Road School in the early 1970's.

Joseph Willis Headmaster
(prior to 1902).

Walton Smith Headmaster
(after 1902).

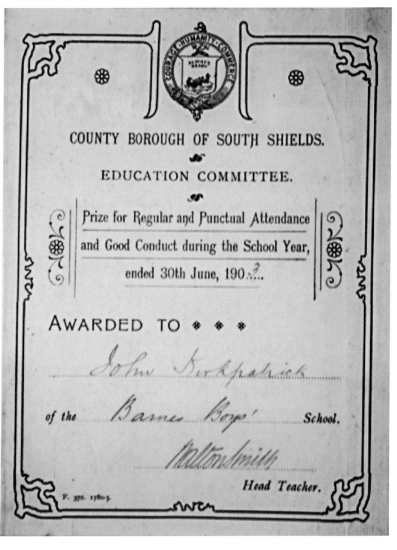

Jack's prize giving book signed by Walton Smith,
30th June 1903.

The fair at Herd Sand with Tynemouth and the North Pier
in the background (circa. 1897).

Donkey Boys at work on Herd Sand with the South Pier
in the background (circa. 1902).

Murphy's Fair at the Market Place with the Town Hall (left)
and St. Hilda's Colliery in the background (circa. 1898).

A Helter Skelter.

James Downey & Sons.

Jack's sister Peggie and her husband Will Balneaves in 1912.

St. Mary's Church and Vicarage (circa. 1906).

The Tyne Dock Gut where Jack saved two children from drowning.

Mortimer Road School in the 1950's.

School records reveal details of Jack's education.

Name	Date of Birth			Address
Dixon Arthur	19	2	91	43 Byron St.
Purdy Henry	12	5	92	66 Chichester Rd.
Pollard Norman	21	11	93	32 Hartington Terr.
Close Thomas	5	12	89	12 Hampden St.
Smith Henry Oliver	18	3	93	2 Derwentwater Terr.
Nicholson George	13	11	92	44 Crofton St.
Smith James	10	8	93	65 Marshall Wallis Rd.
Bruce Albert	9	10	93	238 John Williamson St.
Seago Fred	12	9	89	97 Eglesfield Rd.
Wilson John	2	10	93	178 Eldon St.
Voyce William	27	6	90	5 St. Jude's Terr.
Weightman Christopher	23	7	92	281 Sth. Frederick St.
Barrasford Thomas	4	7	91	105 Commercial Rd.
Miller James	25	12	92	170 Palmerston St.
Morrell John	24	7	91	114 Corporation St. ~~53 West Walpole St.~~
Hughes William	19	10	91	74 H. S. Edward St.
Robson Wilfred	14	11	91	187 Sth. Frederick St.
Kirkpatrick John	6	7	92	141 Sth. Frederick St.
Peacock James	5	1	92	149
Kirby Robt	16	11	90	360 John Williamson St.

The Admissions Register for Mortimer Road School,
29th June 1903.

Jack's horse Andrew in the back lane of South Palmerston Street (circa. 1907).

A small rowing boat takes to the waters of Tyne Dock.

The grand opening of Frenchman's Fort in June 1903.

Frenchman's Fort shortly before the outbreak of WW1.

Jack and his 'Territorial' mates at Knott End Camp,
Fleetwood, June 1909.

Alf Robertson (left) was with Jack (right) at Knott End Camp.

The officers of the 4th Northumbrian (County of Durham)
Howitzer Brigade including Capt. V. Grunhut, Capt. F. M.
Armstrong, Lieut.-Surgeon Henry Goudie, Capt. R. J.
Adams and Capt. Robert Chapman (circa. 1912).

Soldiers leaving Bolingbroke Hall, H.Q.
of the 4th Durham Battery (circa. 1915).

A postcard sent by Jack from Genoa to his sister Annie,
2nd November 1909.

The magnificent Campo Santo Cemetery in Genoa, 1909.

The Canty Bay Hotel run by Jack's half brother
Bob Kirkpatrick (circa. 1905).

Bob Kirkpatrick (2nd from the left) with family and friends.

The Man with the Donkey at Gallipoli.

Jack's sister Annie and his mother Sarah in mourning.

The statuette of a Shields Hero.

A WW1 Recruiting Poster.

Robert Ford, Freemason.

Jack's elderly mother Sarah.

Rev. T. P. Williams (centre) at the unveiling
of St. Mary's War Memorial.

Jack's sister Annie with a copy of Captain Fry's letter
at Mortimer Road School, 1957.

St. Mary's War Memorial bearing the name Kirkpatrick J.S.

The Kirkpatrick/Simpson headstone in Harton Cemetery.

The statue of John Simpson Kirkpatrick in his home town.

The statue of Jack with the old Marine School
(now The Kirkpatrick bar) in the background.

TEN

THE MAN OF THE HOUSE

In the summer of 1905 Jack went to work for a dairyman called Fred Pattinson (b. 1869). He operated from the backyard of his house at 52 Bertram Street, further up the road from the Kirkpatrick's. Jack's mother bought her milk from Pattinson's (or Patta's, as it was known locally) and no doubt helped her son secure his first job. The fact that Jack had experience of handling donkeys would have impressed Fred, since the majority of milk was delivered by horse and cart.

Prior to moving to Tyneside, Fred Pattinson's ancestors had been dairymen on the Naworth Castle Estate near Carlisle as far back as 1803. Initially he operated from 12 Bertram Street (1897-1901) and delivered milk in and around the Tyne Dock area, while his older brother Joe was a dairyman in Jarrow. According to an advertisement in *The Gazette*, Pattinson's Naworth Castle Dairy supplied 'the purest new milk at 4d a quart'. Fred was a gentle giant of a man: he was 6ft 2" tall, had a full head of jet black hair and a moustache. His love of animals (especially horses) was legendary and over the years his milk floats took part in many a street carnival. Fred was a regular visitor to horse fairs where he purchased ponies and sold them through advertisements in the *The Gazette*. In June 1902 he took part in the Coronation Day Horse Procession to celebrate the coronation of Edward VII, alongside Mr. George and his donkeys. Fred entered one his ponies in the 'Milk-cart Pony Class', which was confined to those animals bringing milk to South Shields.

Fred and his wife Mary attended Sunday outings (or charabancs) organsied by the Laygate Presbyterian Church in Frederick Street. The couple had seven children: Lillian, Ruby, Guinevere, Frederick, Mona, Doris and John. Lillian Pattinson (b. 1892) had attended Barnes Road Infants School with Jack and the two became good friends when he worked for her father. Jack obviously thought a lot of Lillian because he acquired a pet Yorkshire Terrier and named her Lil. The Pattinson's were great animal lovers and always spoke favorably of Jack and the Kirkpatrick family. Tragically, Fred drowned in the river off Tynemouth in 1928. However, his widow Mary (who was looked after by her spinster daughter Lillian) lived to be one hundred years old. Lillian never forgot the young Jack Kirkpatrick and was proud of the fact that he named his pet dog after her.

Jack's working day started at five o'clock in the morning. Trains would arrive at High Shields railway station with milk churns from dairy farms as far away as Carlisle in Cumbria and Dumfries on the Scottish border. Fred's quota was loaded onto his horse and cart, and taken to the backyard at Bertram Street. The large 17 gallon milk churns were then poured into much more manageable 5 gallon hand churns and milk cans with handles for lifting. While Fred went out with a milk float to make deliveries to his regular customers, Jack initially pushed a hand cart around the back lanes; ringing a bell and calling out 'Milko', the traditional call of a Geordie milkman. This would bring the women and children out of their houses with jugs and various receptacles for filling. Jack would scoop the milk from a hand churn with a ladle fitted with a half pint or pint measuring can. He had to keep his wits about him, since Fred Pattinson insisted on cash and didn't allow 'tick'. If Jack was foolish enough to believe a customer's sob story which ended with "I'll see you alright at the end of the week", he had to pay any defaulting money out of his own wages. Not surprisingly, Jack soon developed a thick skin when it came to dealing with the various characters on his round.

At this time the back lanes were the workplace of at least a dozen types of hawkers and tradesmen including the knife grinder, the fish girl, the firewood man, the coalman and the children's favourite the rag and boneman. Jack's route took him around the streets of the neighbouring Deans council ward. It was mainly along the back lanes of Alexandra, Francis and Florence Street, as well as along Conway Terrace, Temple Street, Dean Road and some of the houses of John Williamson Street. At this time Jack was followed on part of his milk round by a Shields lad called James Conway (b. 1902). The young Jim lived at the aptly named Conway Terrace off Dean Road. He was only four years old when he accompanied Jack, since he was too young to attend school.

Pattinson's also delivered milk to commercial premises including a shipping butcher called Andrew Anderson of nearby Corstorphine Town. (The latter 'street name' commemorated local businessman Robbie Corstorphine). Andrew Anderson employed an assistant by the name of John Shaw (b. 1885) to row out onto the river in a small sculling boat with orders of meat, milk and eggs. On 26th May 1906 a vessel called the Bride was berthed at the Coble Dene Buoys, down stream from Tyne Dock. The Bride was an iron screw brig, built in 1879 in Hull for Brownlow & Co. and later purchased by the Wilson line. She was laden with esparto grass (used in the making of paper or cordage) and was waiting to unload before leaving for Malaga. An order was placed with Anderson's for some provisions and John Shaw made the delivery with a very special passenger onboard. Many years later he told *The Gazette* the following story about Jack, who at the time was living with his parents and two sisters at Bertram Street.

> He used to come to Andrew Anderson's to get milk orders and he asked me on one occasion to be allowed to go with me in the boat and I said 'Yes'. He left his milk can near the first stairs at Tyne Dock, while he went with me. I remember that it was blowing pretty hard on the river, when the boy Kirkpatrick fell overboard while we were close to a ship called the Bride. I tried to pull him out of danger but he slipped back into the water. When ultimately I got him back in the boat the first words he used were 'Look at my tabs'. I said, "Never mind your tabs man, it's your life you've got to think about." He was holding a penny packet of Woodbines. They were soaked with the water!

John Shaw concluded his story with the following poignant remark:

> I have often thought since, that the life of John Kirkpatrick was spared that he might save the lives of others. I shall always remember him with kindly feelings.

At the age of fourteen Jack was put in charge of a horse drawn milk float, a wooden cart that partly resembled a chariot. Jack stood on a raised platform holding the reins with the milk churns positioned either side of him. It had an open back, about a foot from the ground, so he could easily step on and off to serve customers and make deliveries. His horse was a dappled grey pony called Andrew. Once again, he demonstrated his natural way with animals and according to Annie her brother used to talk to Andrew as if he was human. Like most 'milk horses' Andrew would keep a close eye on his master as he delivered the milk, obeying his every command. However, when Andrew got to one particular place on the round he became an immovable object, this was his feeding place. Jack quickly placed a cloth nosebag, filled with oats, over Andrew's head and after devouring the contents he was his usual obedient self.

Jack finished his milk round at midday, but on returning to Pattinson's backyard his work was far from over. Fred was a stickler for cleanliness since this was before the advent of sterilized milk and sealed bottles, and milk could easily be contaminated. The 17 gallon milk churns needed to be cleaned as did the smaller hand churns, milk cans and measuring scoops. Jack then had to take Andrew and his cart to stables at the nearby West Park Allotments off Dean Road. Finally, he'd feed and groom Andrew but presumably this was more 'a labour of love' than a chore. Jack was so attached to Andrew that he persuaded someone, most probably his brother-in-law Will, to take a photograph of his four legged friend. From time to time Jack took Andrew to a local blacksmith to be re-shoed and

Annie recalled that he cherished one of his old shoes as a keepsake. During the winter months when the cobbled back lanes were covered by a treacherous layer of ice, Fred hammered metal studs into Andrew's shoes for extra grip. Over the next three years Jack and his trusted friend went about their work come rain or snow.

While working the streets of Tyne Dock and the Deans Jack became friends with a lad called John Fenwick (b.1891). John (also known as Jack) worked for his father J. Fenwick Snr., a cartman proprietor. The father and son would hire out their services, initially transporting goods by hand cart but later by horse and cart. They eventually built up a business hiring carts (or barrows) and it was known locally as Fenwickies Barra's. Throughout 1906 and 1907 the electrification of the tramway service caused considerable inconvenience to the townsfolk including the two Jack's. A number of the cobbled roads they traversed on a daily basis were dug up for the construction of tram lines including South Eldon Street. However, it didn't stop them from calling out to one another and meeting up in a back lane for a smoke and a bit of a yarn. As a result of working on his own, without supervision, Jack developed an independent streak which stayed with him for rest of his short life.

Jack enjoyed his job, but life wasn't easy for the young breadwinner of the Kirkpatrick household. His letters from sea recall the hardship the family endured after his father's working career came to an end, including the time he stole a duck one Christmas. This escapade most probably happened as he went to and from the West Park Allotments with Andrew. The wooden huts of the allotments were situated on a bank overlooking the West Park Lake (known locally as the duck pond). The ducks had a habit of straying from the water in search of scraps of food and presumably Jack saw an opportunity to bring some Christmas cheer to the Kirkpatrick household. In the early morning darkness he 'bagged' a duck and rode home on his milk float.

By 1907 Fred Pattinson had moved his dairy business to bigger and better premises, not far from the Kirkpatrick's old house in South Frederick Street. It was known locally as Patta's Milk Shop and Lillian Pattinson worked behind the counter, serving customers with milk and other provisions. Over the next couple of years Jack's milk round took him further afield including making deliveries to more of the businesses on the riverside. During this time Jack made the acquaintance of an enterprising engineer called Robert Ford of Devonshire Street, Tyne Dock. Robert was works manager for Newton & Nicholson's of Commercial Road and would eventually set up his own engineering company with his brother Arthur. In common with many of the skilled tradesmen, managers and local business fraternity, the Ford brothers were members of the Lord Barnard Lodge of Freemasons at Whitehead Street, Tyne Dock. Other members included John Aird Campbell (a grocer, who later became a town councilor), J. Newby (a haulage contractor) and a well known family of blacksmiths called Plater from John Williamson Street. Frederick James Plater (b. 1871) was a sergeant in the town's Royal Garrison Artillery Volunteers and like other Non-commissioned officers (NCO's) he acted as an unofficial recruiting officer for the unit. Jack, the local milkman, obviously made an impression on Robert Ford and his fellow masons, since many years later they would pay their own tribute to him.

ELEVEN

GUNNER KIRKPATRICK

In 1908, while working as a milkman, Jack enlisted as an Artillery Gunner in the newly formed Territorial Force (later known as the Territorial Army). Created by Richard Haldane, the Secretary of State for War, the Territorial Force replaced the three existing volunteer forces: the Militia, the Yeomanry and the Volunteers. All of these had unique identities, but lost them in the reorganization becoming territorial units of army regiments. The Territorial Force remained a part-time form of soldering whose stated role was home defence and men were not obliged to serve overseas. However, come the First World War most of Jack's former colleagues volunteered for active service and saw action in France. In April 1908 the town's volunteers (originally called the 3rd Durham Volunteer Artillery) ceased to be. They were reorganized to form the newly created 4th Northumbrian (County of Durham) Howitzer Brigade, Royal Field Artillery (T). The latter consisted of the 4th Durham Battery with an Ammunition Column and Headquarters at South Shields and the 5th Durham Battery at Hebburn, further along the river.

The 3rd Durham Volunteer Artillery was formed in 1860 following the threat of a French invasion by Napoleon III. Over the years they developed into a coastal defence unit with batteries high up on Trow Rocks, overlooking the mouth of the

Tyne. In 1887 a revolutionary coastal defence gun was placed at Trow Point. The Clarke Maxim 'disappearing' gun was designed to be raised and lowered, enabling it to be fired then reloaded out of sight of enemy ships. Although test shots were fired, it was deemed unsuitable and the gun was removed from service. The Volunteers operated from Trow Point until the eventual construction of Frenchman's Fort further along the rocky coastline at Frenchman's Bay (so called because in 1888 a French ship had grounded there). In 1889 the various volunteer artillery corps throughout the country were allotted to garrison divisions and the 3rd Durham's became Royal Garrison Artillery (RGA) Volunteers.

In the summer of 1903 when Jack was eleven, what seemed like the entire population of South Shields took to the streets. It was the opening of Frenchman's Fort by the 70 year old, Commander-in-Chief of the British Army, Lord Roberts VC; a hero of the Indian Mutiny and the Boer War. Earlier in the day he'd inspected the Clifford's Fort battery at Tynemouth Castle before crossing the river, where he was met at the Market's ferry landing stage by the Mayor, Councillor James Grant, together with some veterans of the Boer War. The party moved on to the Town Hall and Lord Roberts addressed a vast crowd gathered in the Market Place. The carriage and its occupants then proceeded down a packed King Street and along to the new fort at the coast, where Lord Roberts inspected the 3rd Durham Volunteers, R.G.A.

Frenchman's Fort had been several years in the making and was situated high up on the cliffs of Frenchman's Bay with a nearby tented camp, acting as a training base. The plan being, that during hostilities the fort would be manned by volunteers with a small 'stiffening' of regular Royal Garrison Artillery. The buildings of the fort comprised an outer wall with a scattering of pill boxes and observation posts. A large subterranean chamber hollowed out of the cliff top, protected by thick layers of concrete and rock, was used as sleeping accommodation for the young gunners. The fort's ordnance was made at Elswick Ordnance Works in Newcastle. It consisted of two 6-inch quick firing, breach-loading guns weighing 6 tons each. Both were capable of firing four rounds a minute and had a range of 7 to 8 miles. A further 9.2 inch gun (weighing 28 tons) was capable of firing every 45 seconds and had a similar range. This produced the following dark observation by an unnamed observer, "The guns could easily fire a shell across the river and into Blyth."

Haldane's formation of the Territorial Force was not without its critics because many volunteers resented the disbandment of their old units. In June 1908 the Secretary of State for War declared he was "quite satisfied with the number of units formed and the number of men already enrolled", even though nationally the numbers fell short. And what was true of the whole country could be said with even greater truth of South Shields, since it changed from being a coastal defence unit to a mobile howitzer brigade for fighting inland. The authorised strength of the 4th Durham (Howitzer) Battery at South Shields was set at 220 officers and men. By June only 120 had been enrolled, but the local Durham County Territorial Association was confident they would make up the numbers in the near future. One new recruit was William Voyce (aged 18), a classmate of Jack's from Mortimer Road School. William was living at St. Jude's Terrace and working as an apprentice pattern maker when he enlisted as a Horse Driver.

Throughout the autumn of 1908 *The Gazette* was full of stories concerning Haldane's newly created Territorial Force and the publicity swelled the ranks of the 4th Northumbrian's. Jack joined up alongside William Voyce and other men of all ages and occupation's, no doubt for a sense of adventure. The new recruits included Louis Halliday (a coal cutter, aged 19), Joseph H. Flemming (a shipyard joiner, aged 32), William Dinington (a store manager, aged 27), John W. Jordison (an engineer, aged 32), Alexander R. Clarkson (a boilersmith, aged 23), Alf Robertson (a farrier & blacksmith, aged 34), Sidney H. Wilson (a machinist, aged 22), Henry S. Purvis (a moulder, aged 32) and George D. Lazenby (a master baker, aged 30).

The minimum age for a gunner was stipulated as eighteen and Jack lied about his age to enlist. He was only sixteen but looked much older, since three years of lifting milk churns had given him a muscular physique. He underwent a medical examination and was passed fit for service by the brigades' medical officer Dr. Henry Goudie. Jack was put through his paces every Monday and Friday evening at the impressive Drill Hall in Bolingbroke Street; built in 1884 as the headquarters of the 3rd Durham Volunteers. Complete with offices and a large parade ground Bolingbroke Hall, as it became known, was considered to be one of the largest drill halls in the country. As a Gunner he was assigned to a battery section and in his first year he had to perform 45 gun drills and attend 15 days annual training in camp. In common with a lot of the men, the prospect of a fortnight away from the drudgery of work was a factor in Jack's decision to join the Territorials. His uniform was issued to him by the County Durham Territorial Association and he only received pay when under canvass.

On Saturday 12th June 1909, Jack and the rest of the 4th Northumbrian Howitzer Brigade embarked on a fortnight training camp. Their destination was the Lancashire village of Knott End near Fleetwood, over one hundred miles away on the north west coast. An advanced party had left the town on Wednesday under the command of Captain F. M. Armstrong, while the main force paraded at Bolingbroke Hall at 1.30pm and were inspected by Colonel James Drummond, commanding the brigade. Among the officers going to camp were Captain Victor Grunhut, Lieutenants A. and R. T. Coulson, Lieut.-Surgeon Henry Goudie, Veterinarian-Lieut. J. R. Crone and Captain (& Adjutant) R. J. Adams (R.F.A.). Captain Robert Chapman was also present but remained at Headquarters to oversee the day to day running of things, while the brigade were at camp.

According to *The Gazette*, 'The men of the 4th Battery were in marching order with rolled coats slung around them, and made an impressive show as they marched from their headquarters to the railway station, where they had a hearty send off from a large crowd of the public'. In all likelihood Jack's mother and sister Annie were in attendance to wave him goodbye. A special train left South Shields at 2.07p.m. taking the officers, NCO's and men; along with their baggage, a dozen horses, four 5-inch howitzers and four wagons. The train stopped at Hebburn to pick up the men and equipment of the 5th Durham Battery together with the following officers: Major

T. H. Higginbottom (Commanding Officer), Captain F. P. Paynter and Lieutenant's R.G. Angus and A.D. Currie. The train proceeded to Barnard Castle and Tebay, and then onto Knott End which was reached by the early evening.

Once at Knott End some confusion was caused by the late arrival of boots, saddles and a partial breakdown of the local transport. However, this was overcome by the organizational skills of Captain Adams and the enthusiasm of the men. The guns and wagons were unloaded and taken to camp, a distance of about a mile from the station, in a very short time. Owing to the efforts of the advanced party under Captain Armstrong the tents were all pitched and horse lines laid off ready for occupation. Fortunately the weather was fine, so the stores and clothing suffered no damage. At the first opportunity Jack sent a comical postcard to his mother, which reflected his Geordie sense of humour. The card entitled 'Camp Life' featured a cartoon drawing of a soldier, pushing a hand cart loaded with bottles of whiskey. It was sub-titled, 'For the Relief of the Garrison'.

Dear Mother

We arrived at Fleetwood at 6.30. We have just been having tea, two jam wedges and a pint of dirty water. I am now going into town so time is precious. It is now 8 o'clock and we have to be in by ten.

I remain, yours truly,

Jack

XXXX

The next day (Sunday 13th June) the usual morning church parade was dispensed with, a great deal of unavoidable work having been done for the safety and well being of the large number of men and horses in camp. In the afternoon a full muster of men and officers paraded to hear the Army Act read in accordance with camp regulations. Colonel James Drummond complimented the men for their good behaviour and exemplary discipline shown under the many difficulties of the first night. He also expressed his satisfaction at the large number attending the training camp. Out of a total of 354 the number of personnel in camp was 302; comprising 266 men, 24 NCO's and 12 officers.

Jack's visit to the village of Knott End was probably the first time he'd left his home town. The camp offered a fine range for big gun practice with ample scope for training manoeuvres away from any populous centre. On Monday and Tuesday each battery was kept busy picking and pairing their team horses, riding and performing gun drills. On Wednesday the brigade began manoeuvres which were carried out until the following week. The 4th Northumbrian's provided part of the artillery component for the British Army's Northumbrian Division, whose Commander in Chief was none other than Lieut.-General Baden-Powell. According to *The Gazette,* the Hero of Mafeking made a surprise visit to the camp, 'he watched each battery come into action and on visiting the horse lines, he seemed very pleased with what he saw'.

A second postcard Jack sent to his mother hasn't withstood the test of time. However, a reply postcard addressed to 'Gunner Kirkpatrick' reads as follows:-

21st June, 1909

Dear Jack,

Mother received your P.C. this morning. There are 8 pigeons in your ducket now, of course including the young ones. I hope that you enjoy yourself on Wednesday. Sarah and I are going to Knutson's house for the afternoon instead of going to the picnic.

Annie

Jack's love of animals which included rabbits, dogs, donkeys and horses, had been extended to keeping pigeons in the backyard at Bertram Street. Many years later Annie would recall, "My brother loved animals and had a way with them." The Knutson family lived in Dean Road and were friends of Jack's sisters.

On Saturday, the 26th June, the brigade were up early and left Knott End on the 8.15 a.m. train to Newcastle. On returning to 14 Bertram Street, Jack was confronted by a scene of devastation. Across the road at number 19, the premises of the Tyne Dock Co-Operative Society was a burnt out shell. According to *The Gazette*, 'A fire had broken out in the early hours of the morning and the residents next door to the Co-Op had to move their furniture out onto the street for fear that the flames would engulf their house'. Jack's mother and sisters witnessed the drama unfold and no doubt told him all about it. He in turn informed them of his brush with celebrity - the visit of Baden-Powell to the Knott End camp.

TWELVE

HIS FATHER'S DEATH

In the summer of 1909 Jack's sister Annie, aged 14, left Westoe Secondary School (later known as the Girls Grammar). Annie was the brains of the Kirkpatrick children; while Jack liked playing cards or dominoes she preferred to read a good book. Annie passed her exams and went to work as a Lady Clerk. Jack would tease his sister about her cushy office job which had a certain status, even though the wages were poor. With Jack and his two sisters working, the family's financial situation was now improving. Sadly, the prospect of better times ahead didn't last long.

On 15th September 1909, Jack's sister Sarah (aged 21) married Samuel Young Christie (aged 22) at the town's Registry Office in Barrington Street. Sam was a shipyard worker (a plater) who found himself 'in and out' of work. He was one of ten children brought up in Taylor Street, not far from Barnes Road School. By 1909 Sam was living with his mother (a widower) and six other siblings in a 'two-up, two-down' house in Pearson Street by the riverside. After marrying Sarah, not surprisingly, he went to live with the Kirkpatrick family at Bertram Street. Letters written by Jack when he eventually made it to Australia reveal his mother wasn't happy with her daughter's choice of a husband. Despite the Kirkpatrick's being poor themselves, she was of the opinion that her daughter could have done better than marry an unemployed shipyard worker. It's possible Sarah was pregnant but subsequently had a miscarriage, since her first child (Edna) wasn't born until 1913. By this time the couple's luck had changed; Sam was working and they were living just around the corner from the Kirkpatrick's at Garwood Street.

The announcement of Sarah's marriage (sometime prior to September) acted as a catalyst for Jack to join the Mercantile Marine, later known as the Merchant Navy. He was soon to be sharing a small four roomed house with his mother and bedridden father, Sam and Sarah, and his sister Annie. Since his father's accident Jack had shared his bedroom with a number of lodgers. However, with the arrival of Sam Christie this extra source of income came to an end. As there were only two upstairs bedrooms and his parents slept downstairs, the newly weds occupied one room while Jack had to share with Annie. Jack's letters from Australia also reveal that his nose was put out of joint by the arrival of his brother-in-law, who was five years his senior. Up until this point, with his father being incapacitated, Jack was effectively the man of the house. The situation was made worse by the fact that his milk round now had to provide for one more mouth to feed because of Sam's patchy work record. Given the circumstances it wasn't long before tempers frayed and the two men locked horns. Jack's sister Sarah naturally took her husband's side and this brought her into conflict with her brother.

To add to the family's woes Jack's oldest sister Peggie was having marital problems. By 1909 the Balneaves' were living in Boldon, a small village on the outskirts of South

Shields, where Will had set himself up as a freelance photographer. Another letter written by Jack from Australia alludes to his brother-in-law being a bit of a ladies' man, so in all likelihood Peggie brought her problems to her mother's doorstep. The two women frequently argued and Jack berated Peggie for causing trouble. Jack's mother didn't want her only surviving son to go to sea but given the overcrowding and bickering, there was no alternative. Furthermore, by joining the Mercantile Marine he could provide her with a monthly allotment from his wages and possibly make a career at sea. Jack would have looked out for a ship requiring a crew by reporting to the Mercantile Marine Office at the Customs House. The fact that his father was a Master Mariner by profession would have stood him in good stead.

After Robert Kirkpatrick's stroke in 1905, which ended his working career, it would appear that his son Bob sent him money whenever possible. Bob had followed in his father's 'nautical footsteps' and became a successful marine engineer. By 1904 he had saved up enough money to secure the position of licensee of the Canty Bay Hotel in North Berwick, where he lived with his family. Canty Bay at the entrance to the Firth of Forth, was a small fishing village hemmed in the rocky coast by an immense headland which rises close behind it. There was a lot more to the tenancy of the Canty Bay Hotel than being a publican and an inn keeper. Bob was also responsible for the neighbouring tourist attraction of the Bass Rock which was situated a mile at sea to the north of the bay, and rose some 300ft above sea level. He was required to ferry visitors to and from 'the Bass' with a small launch called the 'Bonnie Doon'.

Weather conditions made landing on the rock extremely difficult, necessitating the utmost skill and caution in avoiding disaster. As a marine engineer of considerable experience Bob was ideally suited for the task and he was also entrusted by the Commissioners of Northern Lighthouses with sending and receiving signals to and from the lighthouse on 'the Bass'

One might think Bob would have hated his father for walking out on his mother. However, he was fully aware of her drinking problem at this time and the embarrassment she had caused the family. He was grateful to his father for his education and apprenticeship, as well as for the money he'd sent to help support the his younger brother. Bob also knew from bitter experience that there were two sides to every story, when it came to the break up of a marriage. In 1890 he had divorced his wife Mary Black and won custody of his five children on the grounds of her adulterous behaviour when he was at sea. He later married Mary Bell and the couple had two children. Over the years Bob remained on good terms with his father and most probably met up with him, when he sailed into the port of Leith. For obvious reasons he never told his mother Mary about their friendship and as far as she was concerned Robert's whereabouts were a mystery. Bob didn't hold a grudge against Sarah Simpson and she was grateful to him for his financial support.

By the autumn of 1909 Robert Kirkpatrick had suffered a second stroke and his health was fading fast. In all likelihood Sarah wrote to Bob and made arrangements for him to visit his dying father. In order to protect the Kirkpatrick siblings from the shame of their illegitimacy Jack's mother and Bob were 'economical with the truth'. It would appear Sarah told her children that their father had been married before and had a family by his 'first wife', but he had divorced her because she was an alcoholic. Peggie and Sarah were taken aback by the revelation and wanted to know why this had been kept from them. Jack thought nothing of it and when Bob arrived in Shields he struck up a rapport with his half brother, who was 30 years his senior.

On 10th October 1909, Robert Kirkpatrick died, aged 71. The official cause of death was stated as dropsy, an edema (or swelling), often caused by heart disease. Sarah Christie registered the death the next day and stated her father's age as being 65. It would appear that Robert had lied to his children about his age to cover up the fact that he was nearly 20 years older than their mother. In view of the circumstances Jack's mother wanted the funeral to be as low key as possible and a 'death notice' didn't appear in *The Gazette*. Robert was buried on 12th October at Harton Cemetery in the same plot as his daughter Martha. The funeral was overseen by the Reverend G. Clifford Barker of St. Mary's with the service taking place at the cemeteries chapel, and no doubt Bob Kirkpatrick was in attendance.

Jack's mother now found herself unable to claim Robert's life insurance, since she was not legally his wife. It would appear that Jack's older sisters confronted their mother and the shocking truth of their illegitimacy was revealed. The shame of being illegitimate in Edwardian England cannot be overstated. Peggie and Sarah were furious with their mother but Jack was more forgiving and chastised them for upsetting her. At this time Jack's sister Annie was only told that her father had been married before and had a family by his 'first wife'. Annie would not find out until years later that her parents never married. With tensions already running high the situation within the Kirkpatrick household reached boiling point and two days after his father's funeral, Jack went to sea.

THIRTEEN

JACK GOES TO SEA

On 14th October 1909 Jack secured a position as a messroom steward onboard the SS Heighington (tonnage 2,800). She was built in 1891 and owned by J. E. Guthe, Chairman of the West Hartlepool Steam Navigation Company. The Heighington came into the Tyne on the 9th October and underwent repairs at Smith's Dock Company, across the river at North Shields. Two days later she berthed at Tyne Dock and was loaded with a cargo of coal for the short 'Mediterranean run' to the port of Genoa, Italy.

Jack 'signed on' the Heighington at the Mercantile Marine Office at the Customs House. Members of the crew took it in turn to step up to the counter and a shipping clerk wrote down their details in the presence of the vessel's Master, Fitzroy H. Soares. Each man signed on, 'for a journey not exceeding one years duration to any ports or place within 75 degrees North and 60 degrees south latitude, commencing at the Tyne and proceeding thence to Genoa and/or any ports within the above limits, trading in any rotation, and to the end at such port in the United Kingdom as may be required by the master'. Jack signed his name as *'J. Kirkpatrick'* and stated his age as 19 years old, which was a lie as he was only 17. His wage was £2 and 10s per month and he made an allotment of half this amount for his mother to draw while he was at sea. In addition to being the youngest and lowest paid member of the crew, Jack was also the only one who hadn't been to sea.

The Heighington left the Tyne on the 14th October with a crew of 23 men. Almost half were from South Shields with the others from Jarrow, North Shields, Hartlepool and Whitby. As a messman Jack's duties consisted of the maintenance of the officers messroom and the serving of meals to the engineers and mates, under the watchful eye of the ship's steward. In effect Jack did a bit of everything: he was a waiter, a help to the cook, a pantry man, a dishwasher and he brought the officers their tea when they were on duty. Like many a seafarer he sent letters and postcards home, and picked up mail at foreign ports via British Consuls. Jack didn't keep any of the mail he received from family members while at sea, except for a colourful postcard from Annie. Thankfully his mother and sister kept all of his correspondence, making it possible to follow his life at sea with considerable detail.

On reaching Genoa, Jack wrote to his mother acknowledging the receipt of mail and informing her of his new life at sea.

Dear Mother,

I received your welcome letter this morning at 10 o'clock when we arrived, making it a 14 days trip which I quite enjoyed, I can tell you. Now I hope you are keeping your pecker up and not worrying yourself about me for you have no call at all. Here I am having grand weather and little work and plenty of grub, and eating any Gods amount of it. I think I have eaten more in this fortnight than I have eaten for the last six months. I eat enough for two men at meals, still I always feel "ungry". I am getting an appetite like a horse but there is one consolation there is always plenty of grub, more than is used. They do live high in this Messroom they are fed like fighting cocks, I can tell you. I get up at 4.45 in the morning and make the tea and toast for the second engineer and you bet I have my own tea and toast. I then work on till about 1.30 and then I have my afternoon nap. Oh, I have a pretty soft time of it "it is money for nowt" and I get on well with the engineers, they are three fine fellows. If I keep on the way I am going now I will be like a pet elephant by the time I get home, for the sea air is doing me a lot of good.

After we left the Tyne we did catch the weather until we got through The Bay of Biscay, but my she can roll, because she has no balancers on her bottom. The first Sunday after we got out I had a good laugh, they were having dinner when the ship took a big lurch to one side then over came the soup, vegetables, meat and puddings, all on top of the engineers knees and they could not stop them for they were hanging onto the table for all they were worth. They did look dignified scraping all the rubbish off their pants and jackets, and all the plates and dishes was smashed. I can't tell you anything about Genoa yet for I have not been ashore and I am not going ashore till Saturday night. Now Mother about these photos, send them out as soon as you like they will be very welcome.

Next, Jack turned his attention to family members: Annie; Sarah and Sam Christie; Peggie and Will Balneaves and their children Bob, George and Martha. Following the scandalous news of her illegitimacy Peggie had a tempestuous relationship with her mother. Jack, who considered himself the man of the house, tried his best to be an even-handed referee:

I am glad you and Peggie are getting on alright and I hope it will last, and if Peggie gives you any lip give her a thick ear to be going on with till I get home. And Mother don't let your temper get the better of you or I will tell Peggie to give the same to you till I arrive.

Now tell Annie I am very sorry I did not bid her goodbye, but that was no fault of mine as I did not expect to get away so soon, but never mind kid I am going to buy you a new nose in Genoa and send you some post cards so that will make up for it, and thank Will for me for taking them photo's. Now tell Sarah I hope Sam is working. Tell Bob and George that I will not forget that parrot and monkey. I am sorry to hear that Martha is keeping so poorly but she will soon get better.

Jack's final comments reveal the special relationship he had with his mother.

Now Mother you forgot to put the cards and dominoes in my bag, but then that's not surprising seeing the state you were in. But now 'owld lass' you will not have to worry any more for I am happy as a tinty and I don't see why you should not be the same. Now I don't think you will be able to grumble about this letter being a short letter but I am tired now and I am thinking of turning in. Now hoping this finds you all as it finds me and that is in the pink of condition. Now this is about all I have to say at present, so with love to all.

I remain Your loving Son

Jack

X X X X X X X X X X

PS. Now mother keep your heart up and write out again, for we will be here about a week or ten days and send the photos.

On 2nd November Jack sent a postcard to Annie from Genoa. In addition to being her older brother, Jack was also a father figure to Annie.

Dear Annie

I'm sorry I did not bid you goodbye but never mind I expect that we will be home for the New Year. Now I do hope that you are getting on alright at work and that you are a good girl to your mother or else you will catch it when I get home. Now this is the 2nd and I have not been ashore yet as you have to pay for the boat, but I am going ashore on Sunday to the cemetery. It is the finest in the world. Now this is all at present with love.

Jack

XXXX

At the turn of the twentieth century Genoa was the most important seaport in Italy. The city was renowned for its magnificent monumental cemetery, the Campo Santo ('Palace of the Dead') and Jack's next letter reveals how he was taken aback by its grandeur.

November 9th 1909

Dear Mother,

Just a line to let you know that we are leaving Genoa tonight or tomorrow morning bound for Tunis and Sousse on the North coast of Africa, where we will load part of a general cargo at each port for London and Aberdeen. Now Mother I do hope that you are keeping alright and that Sarah and Peggie are being kind to you. Now don't forget that half pay note on Thursday. I am very sorry to hear Peggie is keeping so poorly and I hope that she will soon get better.

I have been to see the cemetery at Genoa. It is a sight worth going to see. There are hundreds of thousands of pounds worth of statues and monuments on the graves, all cut out of marble. They say it is the finest cemetery in the world and I believe it is. It's beautiful. Now on Sunday I was playing in a football match, a team picked out of the ships in the harbour. We played the Genoa College Boys, an unbeaten team and we beat them four to one.

Now Mother if you answer this sharp I will get it at Tunis. Write c/o The British Consul. Now Mother this is about all at present so give my fondest love to all at home and with love to yourself.

I remain Your loving & Affectionate Son

Jack

XXXXXX

Finally, he added a humorous postscript; poking fun at his kid sister and lambasting his mother for sending him a much awaited photograph in which she didn't look very happy.

PS. I hope you received them PCs all right. Now Annie you are a long time in sending that PC. If it does not come to Tunis I will pull your nose for you when I get home. Oh, I forgot to tell you what I thought of the photo's. They are champion but mother I think you might have tried to look a bit pleasanter – you look like you had lost a tanner and found a three-penny dodger. You know I want something better than yourself not worse, for I know you can look better than that photo when you like. Now don't forget to write sharp.

Solong for now.

The North African coastline was full of bustling Mediterranean ports and Jack was fortunate enough to visit a number of them on his journey home. In Algeria there was Bone (now known as Annaba), Philippeville (Skikda), Djidjelli (Jijel) and Algiers; while in neighbouring Tunisia there was Tunis. In his next letter Jack brought his mother up-to-date with the Heighington's busy schedule, before returning to family matters and a letter he'd received from his half brother Bob. In Jack's absence his mother was struggling to claim the insurance money following his father's death. Jack was aware of the problem but he thought the delay was a mere technicality, since his mother had religiously made the insurance payments.

November 16th 1909

Dear Mother

Just a few lines to let you know that we arrived at Tunis on Saturday morning and we are loading barley and locust beans and will next go to Bone instead of Sousse. From there we will go to Philippeville and then to Algiers to load for London and Leith, instead of Aberdeen.

Now Mother I do hope you are keeping all right and that you and Peggie and Sarah are agreeing and making you happy. I forgot to tell you in my last letter that I had a letter from Bob and he tells me that you have not got the insurance yet. Now Mother it is going to be hard times after all the struggling and depriving yourself that you have had to pay it, to be twisted out of it. I'm afraid Bob was right when he said these insurance companies were a swindle but I hope by the time this reaches you that you have got it all right.

The city of Tunis is built on a hill slope leading down to the Lake of Tunis. Jack was quite taken by the place and the local inhabitants, since his letter concludes:-

> I was ashore in Tunis last night with a young Arab, the ships chandlers son, and a nice fellow he is to. He took me all round Tunis. It is a pretty little place and it looks well to see the Arabs dressed in their long white shirts and white turbans. Now mother we expect to be leaving here tomorrow for Bone but I don't think we will get as far as Algiers for we will have our full cargo by then. Now Mother this is all at present so give love to all at home and with best love to yourself.
> I remain, Your Loving Son,
> Jack
>
> PS. I hope Annie has sent that PC, it has not arrived yet.

On 18th November, as the Heighington was leaving Tunis, Jack received the long awaited postcard from Annie with details of his lonely pet dog and some bad news of her own.

> Dear Jack
> Received your PC and hope you will excuse me for not answering it before now but I really have not had time. Pleased to hear you are keeping well & also enjoying yourself. I was finished at the office last Saturday & I'm now at home, but I hope to get something soon. You have never mentioned Lil in any of your letters but she is keeping all right & sometimes she goes to meet you. Mrs. Wood sends her kind love to you and hopes you will not forget her cashmere shawl you promised her. Now dear Jack with love from us all,
> Your loving sister,
> Annie

After leaving Tunis the Heighington called in at a number of Algerian ports including Bone, Philippeville, Djidjelli and Algiers. These fleeting visits together with his absent minded boss, the ship's steward, began to play havoc with Jack's mail.

> Port of Djidjelli,
> November 30th 1909
>
> Dear Mother
> I received those welcome letters and post card as we were leaving Tunis so I could not answer them from that port. So I wrote as soon as we got to Bone and the steward forgot to give them to the old man to post. He put them away in the drawer and never came across them again until we were leaving Phillipeville. So here I was expecting a reply, when my letters had never went. We arrived at Djidjelli this morning. In fact we are not in yet, for we are lying outside waiting for the pilot. So you can see I am taking the first opportunity of writing.

Next, Jack acknowledged receipt of mail from his older sisters. Although Jack argued with Peggie and Sarah he adopted a conciliatory tone towards them, accepting that he too was at fault over the infighting within the family.

> Now Mother I am glad to hear that you are keeping well at home and Peggie tells me she had you out for an afternoon at Sunderland. "Well done" I am glad to hear that you are all keeping up your spirit and keeping your heart up, and Peggie tells me she has never seen you in a bad temper since I went away. Now that is what I call a good change. Tell Sarah that I received her letter alright and I am glad that she is keeping well and sorry that she is not getting plenty of strokes at work, and

tell her that I hope Sam is working and fetching her plenty of quids.

Now tell Annie I received her PC alright and I am very sorry to hear that she had been paid off but never mind kid, I do hope that you will get another canny little job soon. Now Annie, I am sure it will be hard for you when anybody asks what are you working at, you will not be able to blow out your chest and tell them that you are a "Lady Clerk" but never mind kid I am sure some better job will soon turn up.

Now Mother right up to now we have been having splendid weather, better than it was in the summer at England. We are going to Algiers from here and then to London but I will write from Algiers and let you know the London address. Now Mother I think this is all at present so with fondest love to yourself and all, I remain,

Your Loving and affectionate son

Jack

XXXXXX

Jack's stay in Algiers was a brief one but despite the Heighington's hectic schedule, he managed to send a forwarding address to his mother via a few scribbled lines on a postcard. He also requested that she forward his details to Bob Kirkpatrick in Berwick, since he wanted his half brother to know his whereabouts for future letters.

Dear Mother,

Arrived in Algiers today, leaving tonight. My London address is 18 & 19 Great St. Helen's, Hartlepool Steam Navigation Co. Tell Bob my address for I have just had a letter from him. So with love from Jack.

On Monday 13th December the Heighington arrived at London and true to form, Jack was more concerned about his mail than being 'paid off'. Knowing he was on his way home Jack tried to play the part of family peacemaker, albeit in his own blunt way.

December 16th 1909

Dear Mother,

Just a line or two to let you know that I have just received your letter and I am writing back by return of post as you ask. I wrote on Tuesday night home and I see that you have not said anything about receiving it. Now it seems as if my letters are not getting sent, you see I just take them aft and the skipper he stamps them for me and sends them off.

I sent you a letter from Djidelli and a post card from Algiers with the London address on it. I had no time to write more and you have not mentioned receiving neither PC nor letter in your letter. Now it is a bit thick if my letters are not being sent for I will be charged for them just the same when I pay off. I hear we are going to pay off at Leith.

Now Mother tell Annie that I am very sorry to hear that she is so poorly but I hope she will soon get better and tell Sarah that she will not have to get bad now or else she will be making Sam think that he has got an invalid for a wife.

I think I will be getting the chuck when I get to Leith for I hear that they are going to send a lad from the office. I warned he will be coming for about 30 bob or two pound but he will not get a great catch for the engineers and mates do their own washing. The cook said he has never seen a chief engineer doing his own washing until now, but never mind I expect I will be able to get along without their washing.

Now mother I think this is all except that I have a dose of cold since we left Algiers and a sore throat. Now Mother give my love to Sarah and Annie and with love to yourself,

I remain your loving son,

Jack

PS. It is now 3 o'clock - we expect to leave about 4.

PPS. I wrote to Peggie and Bob last night

Jack's last letter was from Leith, where he took the opportunity to walk around the town where his parents had met. He also shed some light on his working relationship with the ship's steward, Thomas Mercer from North Shields.

December 18th 1909

Dear Mother,

Just a few lines to let you know that I received your welcome letters on Saturday night when we arrived. I had four altogether there was two from you and one from Peggie and one from Bob. Now Mother I don't know whether we are going to pay off here or not, or whether we are going to the Tyne or Cardiff to load and pay off.

I had a letter from Bob and he says that he would like to have a visit from me if I can manage it. I was ashore last night and I had a look around Leith. I was in Leith Walk and all over the shop but it was terribly cold. There was a severe frost and this morning and it is snowing but I have got a good stove in the messroom and it heats the place up a treat.

Now tell Annie that I am very glad to hear that she is getting better and I hope by the time I get home that she will be as well as ever again. Tell Sarah that I am hoping that she is feeling better now and tell her that I am very glad to hear that

Sam is working and being good to her and that she is being good to her mother.

Now Mother I do hope that you are keeping well yourself, for mind I am. I'm eating like a horse. The steward and me have a row every afternoon for I gorge and worry all the roast beef that is left at dinner and take the bare bones to cut cold meat and make a stew for the tea. He does growl, I can tell you, but then you see I blame the engineers for eating all the meat and then it is alright. I think we will be paying off here so I will be home for my duck at Xmas. I say, do you remember when I pinched that duck? So, mind you watch it well this time.

I am very fond of poultry. We have had a good few chickens on the voyage but they were about the size of bantams and nothing but skin and bone, but never mind I got my share of them. The first day we had chicken they wolfed the lot but mind they didn't after that I watched them, for I had my wack shoved in the cupboard before I told them dinner was ready, so you bet I had my chicken as well.

Now Mother I think that is all at present. So give my love to all at home and with love to yourself.

I remain, Your Loving Son,

Jack

XXXXXX

On 20th December Jack was discharged from the Heighington at Leith. In all likelihood he met up with Bob Kirkpatrick in North Berwick. There a regular steam passenger service between Leith and Berwick and an excellent railway service between Berwick and Newcastle for an easy passage home. Jack had been very careful with his money while at sea and the balance of wages paid to him was £2 19s 6d. Presumably, after visiting his half brother he made his way back home to spend Christmas and the New Year with his family.

FOURTEEN

FAREWELL TO "CANNY AULD SHIELDS"

On returning home Jack had good reason to feel proud of himself. He had followed in his father's footsteps and went to sea, but more importantly his wages had helped to support his family. Finally, on seeing his old friend John Fenwick (the cartman) he could hold his head high and entertain him with tales of the exotic places he had visited. The Christmas of 1909 may have been a happy time for Jack, but the money he'd earned on the Heighington wouldn't last long. Come the New Year, with the insurance company refusing to make a payment on Robert's policy, the grim reality of the family's financial plight would fuel the infighting within the household. Although Jack's brother-in-law Sam was now working it did little to mend bridges between the two men. In a letter to his mother when he eventually made it to Australia, Jack accused Sam of "trying to rule the roost" when he moved in with the Kirkpatrick's. In the ensuing arguments Jack's sister Sarah took her husband's side, while their mother supported her son.

Jack also had angry exchanges with his oldest sister Peggie, who on visiting the Kirkpatrick household would argue with their mother. It's possible that when Peggie was given marital advice about her husband she threw it back in her mother's face since she had ran off with a married man, albeit her father. In another letter from Australia, Jack berated Peggie for "never having a good word to say about their mother" and threatened to "wring her neck for talking about her". In the meantime Will Balneaves became increasingly concerned about the unsavoury behaviour of his wife's family, which in turn put pressure on Peggies' already strained marriage. Jack's mother had a fiery temper and one can imagine 'she gave as good as she got'. However, Jack was no angel and would feel the sharp edge of his mother's tongue if he was the cause of trouble. Sadly, the fact of their illegitimacy was a constant source of tension between Jack's mother and her two oldest daughters. Once again Jack went to sea, partly to diffuse the volatile situation at home but primarily to provide for his mother.

According to Annie her brother always wanted to go to Australia. Whether or not he was influenced by his father's exploits 'down under' is not known. While visiting the shipping office, looking for a vessel bound for Australia, an unexpected 'arrival' caught the attention of Jack and the rest of the townsfolk. On 28th January 1910 a Norwegian sailing ship, the Alphonse, was driven ashore in heavy seas and gale force winds at Herd Sand near Trow Rocks. The Volunteer Life Brigade managed to get a line onboard, while a lifeboat recued all 29 of her crew. Luckily, only part of her cargo of silver sand was lost to the sea. Over the following weeks crowds of people gathered in the freezing cold to catch a glimpse of the stricken vessel. If Jack dreamed of warmer climes, he didn't have long to wait for his dream to come true.

On 11th February 1910 a steamship called the Yeddo berthed at Tyne Dock, having sailed up from the Thames. She was built in Glasgow in 1901 and owned by A. Weir & Company. The SS Yeddo had a tonnage of 4,563 and was a beast of a vessel compared to the Heighington. The Yeddo was bound for the busy Chilean port of Valparaiso on the west coast of South America. Valparaiso served as a major stopover for ships travelling from Europe via Cape Horn to Australia, prior to the building of the Panama Canal. Her skipper Sydney Robson had tried to engage a Chinese crew in London but due to the Chinese New Year celebrations he found himself short of men for the long voyage ahead.

By now Jack was about 5ft 8" tall, of stocky build and weighed nearly 12 stone. Looking to earn as much money as an unskilled worker could he secured a job as a stoker; undertaking the arduous and dirty work of shoveling coal in the bowels of the ship. Jack joined the Yeddo's crew on the 12th February for an overall voyage 'not exceeding three years', hoping her next port of call after Valparaiso would be Australia. It's interesting to note that he signed on as '*J. S. Kirkpatrick*', thus acknowledging for the very first time that he was a Simpson as well as a Kirkpatrick. Again, Jack lied about his age stating he was 19 when he was only 17. He was the youngest of 12 stokers, all of whom were experienced seamen. Many of the crew were from South Shields including Alex Leslie (aged 50), Thomas Dick (aged 34), David Clark (aged 45) Charlie Andrews (aged 35), Thomas Rogers (aged 59), John Manson (aged 59), Robert Hanson (aged 35), James Eric Anderson (aged 19) and John Robinson (aged 29). Jack was paid the sum of £4 a month and made an allotment, enabling his mother to draw £2 on the 12th day of each month he was at sea.

On 13th February 1910 Jack left Tyne Dock on the Yeddo, unaware that he would never return. It was the end of 'Jack Kirkpatrick the Shields Lad' and the beginning of 'Aussie Jack'; and ultimately 'Simpson, The Man with the Donkey'.

FIFTEEN

AFTERMATH

By the end of September 1915, as well as receiving Captain's Fry's letter of condolence, Jack's mother was also in receipt of newspaper cuttings from Australia regarding her son's heroics. However, apart from the Kirkpatrick family no one from his home town was any the wiser. After all, he was being feted 10,000 miles away as 'Private Simpson of the Australian Army Medical Corps', not as 'Jack Kirkpatrick from South Shields'. Then, out of the blue, a small article taken from the Australian press appeared in *The Gazette*. It told the story of 'a stretcher bearer called Simpson, a hero of Anzac, who figures frequently in the home letters of Australian survivors of the early fateful days after the landing'. Jack's mother bursting with pride and justifiably wanting her son to receive the recognition he deserved, approached *The Gazette* with Captain Fry's letter. On the 3rd October a full page article appeared in the newspaper under the headline, 'How a Shields Hero died in Gallipoli'. The article gave no explanation as to why he'd enlisted under the name Simpson. Jack was referred to as 'John Simpson Kirkpatrick the only son of Mrs. Kirkpatrick of 14 Bertram Street', which of course was not true.

Contrary to popular belief, the fact that Jack jumped ship a few weeks prior to joining the army had nothing to do with his decision to drop the name Kirkpatrick. The army authorities had no way of checking the information provided by thousands of recruits - all that mattered to them was that you passed the medical. The truth of the matter is Jack enlisted in the Australian Army under the name Simpson because he wanted his mother (Sarah Simpson) to be able to draw part of his wages from his bank account. Jack knew full well the problems she had encountered trying to claim the insurance money on his father's policy because she wasn't Mrs. Kirkpatrick. Sadly, as Sarah was born in Spain and had ran away from home, she didn't have a birth certificate. Therefore, she could not prove her identity and this caused a delay in receiving her son's army pay.

Unbeknown to Jack, his childhood playmate Billy Lowes also ended up at Gallipoli serving with the Royal Naval Division. The latter was known as 'Winston's Little Army' because it was founded by Winston Churchill, First Lord of the Admiralty; the architect of the doomed plan to 'force the Dardanelles at Gallipoli'. At the outbreak of the First World War the Reserves of the Royal Navy were found to have a surplus of thousands of sailors even though the warships were fully manned. This war would be conducted mainly on land so there was an obvious solution. In September 1914 the Royal Naval Reserve, Royal Fleet Reserve, the Royal Naval Volunteer Reserve and a brigade of Royal Marines were brought together to form the Royal Naval Division. The naval personnel were hastily retrained to fight on land as infantrymen. Due to Tyneside's importance as a seafaring area, the battalions of the Royal Naval Division were packed with men from the coastal towns of Northumberland and Durham including South Shields.

On 3rd May 1915, under the cover of darkness, able seaman Billy Lowes and the rest of Nelson Battalion toiled up a hillside at Gallipoli to support the battle hardened ANZAC's. According to Billy he was hit by shrapnel in several places including the leg, and in a state of shock was taken down to the beach by a man with a donkey. While recovering in hospital in Egypt he wrote to his parents at John Williamson Street, informing them of his narrow escape. On returning home on leave, Billy's parents showed him *The Gazette* article featuring Jack's heroics at Gallipoli. Billy naturally assumed that his old playmate must have been the man who brought him to safety, although he didn't recognise him at the time. He tried to meet up with Jack's mother but things didn't go to plan. However, he wrote her the following letter from the Royal Naval Division's camp in Blandford, Dorset.

November 26th 1915

Dear Mrs. Kirkpatrick,

I was very sorry that I could not come to see you before I left as I had to leave home on Friday night instead of Saturday, as the train on Saturday would not catch the connections & I would not have got here till Monday, so you will have to excuse me. I arrived here on Saturday at 4pm, & I saw the doctor & he has given me duty & put me in the first class & that means that I will have to go away again, but I am going to see him again in the morning, as my leg is troubling me with the heavy shoes. I don't think much of the doctor that I saw, I will see another one in the morning. I hear that we are going to get either 7 or 10 days at Xmas, so I will pay you a visit. Hoping that you are keeping better, I often think about Jack especially when I tell people about your son saving me & losing his own life after doing so much good work, & if anybody was worthy of a VC it was Jack. I think this is all the news at present & will be sure to see you at the holidays.

I remain,

W. Lowes

Billy Lowes was eventually placed in 'the Reserve' and demobilized in June 1916, returning to his civilian job at Readhead's shipyard. However, it would only be a matter of time before the people of South Shields heard his remarkable story. On 18th October *The Gazette* informed its readers: 'An exhibition of Louis Raemaekers' world famous war cartoons is to be opened in the Public Library Museum in Ocean Road'. The article also described other parts of the exhibition including, 'An exhibit of very great interest to the people of this town is the bronze statuette, The Man with the Donkey, executed by Mr. A. Bertram Pegram. It immortalizes John Simpson Kirkpatrick a native of South Shields'. The story was read by members of the Tyne Dock Masons and some of them visited the exhibition. On hearing that the library wanted to keep the statuette in the town, they approached the artist and purchased it.

On 16th May 1917 the Tyne Dock Masons presented the statuette to Alderman J. W. Henderson, Chairman of the Free Library Committee. According to *The Gazette*, the gathering took place in the Reference Library, which was crowded by the general public. Alderman Henderson was supported in his duties by the Mayor and Mayoress *(Mr. & Mrs. William Allon);* the Mayoress being accompanied by Mrs. Kirkpatrick and her daughter, Miss Kirkpatrick *(Annie)*. Also present were Ambrose Flagg (former superintendant of the town's Marine School) and members of the Tyne Docks Masons including Robert Ford and Councilor John Aird Campbell. After the Chief Librarian Ernest Bailey gave a eulogy of 'Kirkpatrick's heroic deeds at Gallipoli', the presentation of the statuette was made.

Robert Ford addressed the crowd and declared that he had a personal interest in the matter because it had been his pleasure and privilege to be associated with the young Kirkpatrick while he lived at Tyne Dock. He then went on to say that they were delighted to see Mrs. Kirkpatrick and her daughter present and was sure that, although it had its sorrowful side, it was a proud and glorious moment in their lives. A photograph of the statuette was then presented to Jack's mother who was enthusiastically applauded; the Mayoress pinned an Australian Military Badge upon her and presented her with a bouquet of roses. Mrs. Kirkpatrick feelingly thanked the Mayoress for her kind wishes, and assured them that it was a proud day in her life to find her brave son honoured in the way they were doing. Children from Jack's old school of Mortimer Road then sang a song and one of the boys recited the poem 'Play the Game' by Henry Newbolt.

At the end of the proceedings Billy Lowes presented himself at the head table and was invited to address the gathering. Billy told the assembled crowd that he was wounded at Gallipoli on the 3rd May while serving with the Royal Naval Division and that "Kirkpatrick brought me in on his donkey." Without a doubt Billy Lowes was ferried to safety by a man using a donkey, but it may not have been Jack. Unbeknown to Billy, a number of New Zealand stretcher bearers had seen the usefulness of Jack's work and also used donkeys to transport the wounded during the first few days of May. Over the years Billy sang the praises of Jack and always assumed that he hadn't recognised his old playmate because he was in a state of shock.

On 3rd August 1918 Jack's sister Annie (aged 23) married Francis A. Parkin (aged 24), an able seaman in the Royal Navy. The wedding took place at St. Mary's, Tyne Dock and the celebrant was the Rev. T. P. Williams. The couple initially lived with Jack's mother and had two children: Joan Simpson Parkin (b. 1919) and John Simpson Parkin (b. 1921), named after Jack. In January 1922 one of the last acts of 'Daddy Williams' as vicar of St. Mary's, was to unveil a memorial cross to the memory of the members of the parish and congregation who made the supreme sacrifice in the Great War. The stone cross mounted on a large base was designed by local sculptor Thomas Curry and occupied a commanding position on a grass mound in front of the church. On the four panels of the base were inscribed the names of the 182 men of the parish who fell in the war. At the close of the ceremony a large number of wreaths were laid at the foot of the memorial. Jack's name amongst the roll of honour reads as follows: *Kirkpatrick J. S.* With no grave to mourn her son, Sarah would regularly pay her respects by placing a remembrance wreath at the memorial. St. Mary's Church was demolished in 1984 but the memorial parish cross bearing Jack's name is still there.

Tragedy was never far away from the Kirkpatrick family and in January 1925 Annie's husband Francis was lost at sea, when his ship the SS Harrison foundered off the coast of Holland. Annie secured an office job at Newby's Haulage Company and her mother looked after Joan and John. By this time the family had left Tyne Dock and were living in Dale Street, which shared a back lane with Ocean Road. The young John Simpson Parkin would accompany his grandmother to listen to the bands play in the nearby Marine Park; a few hundreds yards away from the beach where Jack worked as a donkey boy. It was while working at Newby's that Annie met Adam Pearson of Garden Lane, who was employed as a cartman. In October 1931 Annie Simpson Parkin (aged 36) married Adam Maddison Pearson (aged 35) at St. Hilda's Church. Adam served with the East Yorkshire Regiment during the war and like Jack he loved animals, especially horses. By all accounts Adam was a quiet hardworking man who was very good to his elderly mother and sisters. The couple didn't have any children, but Adam was a kind and loving stepfather to Joan and John.

On 9th February 1933 Jack's mother died, aged 77. She was buried in the family plot at Harton Cemetery, along with Robert Kirkpatrick and their daughter Martha. By now Annie knew her parents had never married and she was illegitimate. Her mother's 'name & surname' on her death certificate read as follows: '*Sarah Simpson otherwise Kirkpatrick - Spinster*'. Not surprisingly the funeral was a private affair with only Adam, Annie and her two children (John and Joan) in attendance. However, a reporter from the Newcastle Chronicle contacted Annie and a few days later details of Sarah's death appeared under the headline 'Gallipoli Hero's Mother Dies'. Annie told the Chronicle, "Her mother had contracted a chill which resulted in her death while visiting St. Mary's Church on January 3rd, to place a holly remembrance wreath on the war memorial bearing her son's name. On her death bed her last thoughts were of her son and his name was constantly on her lips."

Sadly, until her dying day, Sarah was hard on herself regarding the circumstances of her beloved son's death. She blamed herself (and her past indiscretions) for the infighting within the family which led him to go to sea. Sarah thought that if Jack had not been in Australia at the outbreak of war, he wouldn't have ended up at the killing fields of Gallipoli. However, if Jack had remained in Shields in all likelihood he would have served with his territorial mates in France. Tragically, the town's war memorials bear witness to the victims of the carnage on the Western Front including Jonathan Deaton who taught Jack at 'The Barnes' and his Sunday School friend Robert Hogg.

By the 1950's Jack's old school of Mortimer Road was more responsible for keeping his memory alive than any other public body in the town. His photograph was displayed in the classrooms and the school held an annual memorial service for him. Over the years these services were attended by Annie (now known as Mrs. Simpson Pearson), Billy Lowes and Willie Bowman. Willie had done well for himself and was the Joint Manager of the prestigious Allen's Department Store in Laygate. In July 1956 he donated a trophy to Mortimer Road in memory of his old friend from St. Mary's Sunday School. The trophy became known as the Kirkpatrick Cup and was contested annually at the school's swimming gala, held at Derby Street Baths.

In August 1956 the Reverend Irving Benson arrived in Shields from Australia to research his book 'The Man with the

Donkey'. As a result of an appeal published in *The Gazette* he met with Willie, Annie and Billy at their respective homes. Billy Lowes, who walked with a limp, recalled his remarkable story and showed the clergyman a little linen tag signed by the medical officer the day he was wounded. For obvious reasons Annie didn't tell Benson the truth about her mother and father. She simply said her parents Robert and Sarah Kirkpatrick were Scots who had settled in South Shields. Annie loaned Benson all of the letters Jack had written between 1909 and 1915. Benson selected what he thought were the most interesting letters and edited them, mainly to omit the squabbling between family members. Subsequently, these edited versions appeared in his book. Only one of the letters referring to 'Bob' was published and Benson, like all other authors since, was oblivious to his identity. Annie later donated all of Jack's correspondence and his service medals to the Australian War Memorial in Canberra.

By the end of the 1950's Annie's grown up children Joan and John had left Shields for the South of England and she decided to leave to be close to them. However, before leaving Annie and Adam paid for an elegant marble headstone for the Kirkpatrick/Simpson grave at Harton Cemetery. In addition to remembering her mother, father and sister Martha, she included the following inscription:

John Simpson Kirkpatrick AIF
Killed in Action at Gallipoli
He Gave His Life That Others May Live
Known at Gallipoli as The Man with the Donkey

In Annie's absence the grave was looked after by Adam's sister Mrs. Mary Mason and her family. Annie kept in touch with Mary and over the years she regularly paid for a notice to be printed in *The Gazette*, in memory of her "brave brother".

In 1988, Australia's bicentenary year, a statue of John Simpson Kirkpatrick was erected in Ocean Road; a short distance from the town's museum. It was designed by South Shields artist Bob Olley and was paid for by public subscription. The 2.5m tall, bronze coloured statue was unveiled by the Mayor, Councillor Albert Tate. The brass plaque on the stone plinth bears the inscription:-

John Simpson Kirkpatrick AIF

"The Man with the Donkey"

202 Pte. John Simpson Kirkpatrick

Born South Shields, 6th July 1892

Australian Army Ambulance Corps

Died Gallipoli 19th May 1915

A Hero of the Great War

The statue is situated in front of an impressive Victorian building, originally the Marine School of South Shields built for the training of seafarers. In 1990 it became a public house and was named The Kirkpatrick in his honour. In view of the fact that Jack was a merchant seaman, many local people consider it to be a fitting memorial to the town's most famous son.

In 1988 I was passing the old Marine School and witnessed the unveiling of the statue; never thinking that one day I would write 'The Untold Story of the Gallipoli Hero's Early Life'.

ACKNOWLEGEMENTS

I would like to thank the following people without whom this book would not have been possible: Wendy and Graham Zeller (Wendy's grandmother Sarah was John Simpson Kirkpatrick's sister); Paul Heiser whose great grandmother was John's eldest sister, Peggie; Doug Walton the great grandson of Bob Kirkpatrick, the paternal half brother of John; Ian Claridge the great grandson of Annie Simpson Kirkpatrick (John's youngest sister) and Mrs. Mary Reay (nee Mason) - Annie's niece. I'm particularly grateful to Ian for his permission to reproduce the correspondence of John Simpson Kirkpatrick, kindly donated to the Australian War Memorial by his great grandmother. This includes all of the letters and postcards written by John to his mother and sister Annie on his first sea voyage, as well as the letters written by Captain Fry and Billy Lowes.

I'm also indebted to the late Tom Curran, author of 'Across the Bar: The Story of Simpson', who I corresponded with prior to his untimely death in 2011. Tom kindly sent me his correspondence with Annie's son John Simpson Parkin including photographs and family information which he did not publish.

I'm very grateful to Mrs. Mary Ford (a former Headmistress of Barnes Road School); Ms. Claire Mullane (Head Teacher of Mortimer Community College); Geoff Seagrove (Headmaster of Mortimer Road Primary School) and the granddaughter of dairyman Fred Pattinson (John Simpson Kirkpatrick's employer) who wishes to remain anonymous.

I'd also like to thank the Australian War Memorial (AWM), the National Archive of Australia, the Memorial University of Newfoundland, the National Archive at Kew, the

National Archives of Scotland at Edinburgh, Tyne & Wear Archive, South Tyneside Library Service and South Shields Museum for all their assistance with my research.

A very special thank you goes to Anne Sharp and members of South Shields Local History Group for all their help and support with my research. Thanks also to local writer & historian Robert Crosby; former South Shields librarians Keith Bardwell and Hildred Whale; John Stobbs B.A. (Editor of Northumberland & Durham Ancestry); John and Margaret Macdonald of the Jarrow and Hebburn Local History Societies; Angus Macdonald of South Shields Museum; Jennifer Dunn of the Port of Tyne Authority; local photographers Mary Naughton and Ken Lubi; Kirsty Gordon for her guided tours of Berwick and Leith; Australian Military Researcher Ian Warden; Dr. Gardiner-Medway and Professor John Pearn. I'm also grateful to Grant Malcolm, Lynne Maughan, Tanya Macdonald, Victoria Brown, Geoffrey Ford, Ronald Heron, Eileen Tebble, Dianne Thompson, Malcolm Maclean, Edna Patterson, John Bage, Helen Close, Ken & Joyce Brady, John Woodmass, Gordon Walker, Barry Hails, Doreen & Margaret Bairnison, Bob Olley, Stuart Conway, Phil & Tom Mulholland, Jean Stokes, Ernest Lusher, Catrin Galt, Norman Paxton, Stephen Landells, Bill Richardson, Jim Capstick, Stanley Blenkinsop, George Wanless, Pat Rundle and Ken Sumner.

Finally, I'm very grateful to Janis Blower (Features Editor of the Shields Gazette) for publicising my appeals for information, as well as for her fascinating articles regarding the history of the town. These together with the Archive of the Shields Gazette, the oldest provincial newspaper in the world, have become a valuable research tool for historians, scholars and writers alike.

BIBLIOGRAPHY

Secondary Sources:

Hodgson, George, *The Borough of South Shields from the earliest period to the close of the nineteenth century. Andrew Reid & Co. Ltd, 1903.*

Blower, Janis, *Banks of the Tyne, A Shields Gazette Publication, 1977-79.*

Hogg, Brigadier O.F.G., *The History of the 3rd Durham Volunteer Artillery 1860-1960. Northern Press Ltd. 1960.*

McClelland, Arthur, *From Tyne to Tsar, University of Sunderland Press, 2007.*

Landells, Stephen, *Rescues in the Surf, Tyne Bridge Publishing, 2010.*

Benson, Sir Irving, *The Man with the Donkey, John* Simpson *Kirkpatrick, Hodder & Stoughton, London, 1965.*

Curran, Tom, *Across the Bar: The Story of Simpson, The Man with the Donkey, Omigos Publications, Brisbane 1994.*

Cochrane, Peter, *Simpson and the Donkey: The Making of a Legend, Melbourne University Press, 1992.*

Rimmer, Michael R., *The Man Who Loved Animals: John Simpson Kirkpatrick, 1987.*

Walsh, Tom, *The Man and the Donkey, Auckland, New Zealand Walsh Printing Co., 1948.*

Primary Sources:

Personal recollections, letters, documents & photographs of the descendants of John Simpson Kirkpatrick's family and friends.

Australian War Memorial, Canberra – Letters, postcards & photographs of John Simpson Kirkpatrick, his mother Sarah and sister Annie.

South Tyneside Libraries - The Archive of the Shields Gazette, cemetery records, maps, street directories and photographs (www.southtynesideimages.org.uk).

National Archive of Australia – Military Records.

Memorial University of Canada, Newfoundland – Official Crew Agreements.

Scottish National Archive, Edinburgh - Records of the London & Edinburgh Shipping Company and Official Crew Agreements.

Tyne & Wear Archive, Newcastle upon Tyne - School Log books, Admission Registers & Attendance Records.

Official Websites – Certificates of Births, Deaths & Marriages, Census Returns and Military Records.

www.nationalarchives.gov.uk
www.scotlandspeople.gov.uk
www.familyrelatives.com
www.findmypast.co.uk
www.ancestry.co.uk

INDEX